Irish Family History on the Web

A Directory

SECOND EDITION

Stuart A. Raymond

FEDERATION OF FAMILY HISTORY SOCIETIES (PUBLICATIONS) LIMITED

Published by:
Federation of Family History Societies (Publications) Ltd.,
Units 15-16, Chesham Industrial Estate,
Oram Street, Bury,
Lancashire BL9 6EN

in association with
S.A. & M.J. Raymond,
P.O.Box 35,
Exeter,
EX1 3YZ
Phone (01392) 252193
Email: samjraymond@btopenworld.com
Webpage: www.samjraymond.btinternet.co.uk/igb.htm

ISBNs:
Federation of Family History Society: 1-86006-183-4
S.A. & M.J. Raymond: 1-899668-38-1

First published 2001
Second edition 2004

Printed and bound by the Alden Group, Osney Mead, Oxford OX2 0EF

Contents

Introduction

A vast amount of information concerning genealogy and family history is now available on the internet. Surfing the net can be a very productive process for the researcher; it can, however, also be very frustrating. There are thousands of genealogical web sites worth visiting, but the means for finding particular relevant sites are very poor. Search engines frequently list dozens of relevant sites, but not the ones required. 'Gateway' sites are not always easy to use. Links are not always kept up to date. It is easy for relevant sites to escape attention.

I hope that this directory will provide at least a partial means for overcoming these problems. It is intended to help you identify those sites most relevant to your research. The listing is, inevitably, selective. I have only included those sites likely to provide you with useful information. Sites devoted to particular families are excluded: a listing would occupy at least a whole volume. I have also excluded passenger list sites dealing with single voyages: again, a full listing would be extensive. Sites of general interest, e.g. search engines, maps, *etc.*, are also excluded. Many of the sites I have listed, and especially those in chapters 1, 7 and 8, can be used to find sites excluded from this directory.

Beginners should also consult:

CHRISTIAN, PETER. *Finding genealogy on the internet.* 2nd ed. David Hawgood, 2002. This book offers many suggestions to help you improve your surfing techniques.

It should be noted that **http:** should be prefixed to all URLs in this directory.

This listing is as up-to-date as I have been able to make it. However, new web pages are being mounted every day, and URLs change frequently. Consequently, it is anticipated that this directory will need frequent updating. If you are unable to find a site listed here, then you should check Cyndis List or one of the other gateways listed in chapter 1; the probability is that the site has moved to another address. Alternatively, search words from the title - or the URL - on a search engine such as www.google.com. It is frequently the case that sites which have not been found directly can be found in this way.

If you know of sites which have not been listed here, or which are new, please let me know so that they may be included in the next edition of this directory. Over 700 pages are new to this edition; in particular, there are much more extensive listings of sites relating to births, marriages and deaths, and to monumental inscriptions.

My thanks go to Cynthia Hanson, who has typed most of this book, to Bob Boyd, who has seen it through the press, and to the officers of the Federation of Family History Societies, who accepted it for publication.

Stuart A. Raymond

1. Gateways, Search Engines etc.

There are a variety of gateways and search engines for Irish genealogists. One of the most useful is Genuki, which itself provides a great deal of general information. Cyndis list is the major international gateway; it has an American bias, but nevertheless provides numerous links to Irish sites. Quite a number of sites offer similar help, although the 'international' ones tend to be biased towards U.S. genealogy. General search engines are not listed here; they may be found on Cyndis List, or by accessing some of the other sites listed below.

- Genuki Ireland
  www.genuki.org.uk/big/irl

- Genuki Book by David Hawgood
  www.hawgood.co.uk/genuki/index.htm
  A useful description of Genuki contents, also published in book format as HAWGOOD, DAVID. *Genuki: UK and Ireland Genealogy on the Internet.* David Hawgood / Federation of Family History Societies, 2000.

- Cyndis List of Genealogy Sites on the Internet: Ireland & Northern Ireland
  www.cyndislist.com/ireland.htm
  The most extensive listing of genealogical websites on the internet, which has also been published in book format:
  HOWELLS, CYNDI. *Cyndis's list: a comprehensive list of 40,000 genealogy sites on the Internet.* Baltimore: Genealogical Publishing, 1999.

- Roots Web Genealogical Data Cooperative
  www.rootsweb.com
  Home to thousands of genealogical mailing lists, the Genweb project, web sites, *etc., etc.* American bias, but also of Irish interest.

- Ireland Genealogical Projects: The Original Ireland Gen Web Project
  irelandgenealogyprojects.rootsweb.com
  Lists county pages, query pages, *etc.*

See also:
- The Ireland Gen Web Project
  www.irelandgenweb.com/

There are a variety of other gateway sites:
- The Celtic Connection
  www.geocities.com/Heartland/Prairie/8088/ire.html
  Gateway mainly to county websites

- Genealogy Ireland~Eire~History
  www.members.tripod.com/~Caryl__Williams/Eire-7.html

- Genealogy Resources on the Internet: Irish Genealogy
  www-personal.umich.edu/~cgaunt/irish.html
  Gateway

- General Ireland Genealogy Links & Chat
  members.shaw.ca/justgen/genire.htm
  Gateway

- Helm's Genealogy Toolbox: Ireland
  www.genealogytoolbox.com/ireland.html
  Gateway

- Ireland Genealogy Links
  www.genealogylinks.net/uk/ireland/
  Gateway

- Ireland: Irish Genealogy Pages
  www.scotlandsclans.com/ireland.htm

- Irish Ancestral Pages
  www.geocities.com/irishancestralpages
  Includes various databases

- Irish Family History: specific Irish Genealogy Sites
  www.nzsghamilton.co.nz/ireland.htm
  Gateway

- Irish Genealogy
  www.daddezio.com/irishgen.html
  Gateway

- Irish Genealogy Links
  www.geocities.com/SiliconValley/Haven/1538/irish.html

- Irish Genealogy on the Net
  irishgenealogy.net/
  New gateway.

- Irish Heritage & Genealogy Links
  indigo.ie/~rfinder/Links.html
  Gateway

- Irish Insight:
  The A to Z of Irish Genealogy
  www.irish-insight.com/a2z-genealogy

- Irish Resources on the Internet
  www.genealogy.com/30__links.html
  Brief introduction

- Searcher: the Irish Genealogy Search Engine & Directory
  www.ireland-information.com/irishgenealogy/

- UK Genealogy. Ireland Research
  www.ukgenealogy.co.uk/ireland.htm
  Covers Eire and Northern Ireland

- What's What in Irish Genealogy
  indigo.ie/~gorry
  Gateway to quality sites

Many Irish genealogical sites may be found by commencing at one of:
- Discover Ireland Genealogy Web Ring
  www.accessgenealogy.com/rings/ire

- Discover Northern Ireland Genealogy Webring
  www.accessgenealogy.com/rings/nire/index.htm

For a gateway to Irish genealogy in Canada, visit:
- Irish Genealogy in Canada
  layden-zella.tripod.com/IrishGen.index.html

If you want to place your research in the wider context of Irish history, see:
- Irish History on the Web
  larkspirit.com/history/

Sites which are no longer current may still be read at:
- Internet Archive Wayback Machine
  web.archive.org/web/web.php

2. General Introductions to Genealogy

Numerous general guides to Irish genealogy are available on the internet; most provide similar basic guidance. Many family history society sites (chapter 4 below) have beginners' guides; so do many of the county pages listed in chapter 7. Some of the pages listed below are extensive - especially those from major institutions.

- Centre for Irish Genealogical and Historical Studies
  homepage.tinet.ie/~seanjmurphy
  Includes 'Directory of Irish genealogy', *etc.*

- Directory of Irish Genealogy
  homepage.eircom.net/~seanjmurphy/dir/

- Family Search Ireland Research Guidance
  www.familysearch.org/Eng/Search/RG/frameset__rg.asp
  Guide from the Latter-Day Saints - select 'Ireland'

- Fianna Guide to Irish Genealogy
  www.rootsweb.com/~fianna
  Extensive, including county pages, and many databases

- Finding Your Ancestors in Ireland
  www.genealogy.com/genealogy/4__pocket.html?Welcome=1083401080
  For the descendants of emigrants; includes brief notes on sources in Australia, Canada, New Zealand, the U.S.A. and the U.K.

- From Ireland
  www.from-ireland.net
  Extensive new site

- How to Trace Your Family Tree
  proni.nics.gov.uk/research/family/family01.htm

- Ireland Research Outline
  www.familysearch.org
  Click 'Search', select 'Research Helps', choose places beginning with I, and click title.

- Irish
  www.genealogy.com/00000374.html
  Brief introduction

- Irish Abroad
  www.irishabroad.com/YourRoots/

- Irish Ancestors
  scripts.ireland.com/ancestor/

- Irish Ancestors: Irish Times
  www.ireland.com/ancestor/
  One of the best sites; hundred of pages

- Irish Ancestors.net
  freepages.genealogy.rootsweb.com/~irishancestors/

- Irish Genealogy: search for your roots
  www.goireland.com/Genealogy/

- Irish Genealogy and History Articles
  globalgenealogy.com/globalgazette/irish.htm
  Collection of articles, some listed here separately.

- The Irish Genealogy Homepage of Sean E. Quinn
  freepages.genealogy.rootsweb.com/~irishancestors/
  Introduction; includes guides to various sources.

- Irish Research
  www.genealogy.com/4__irsrcs.html
  Brief introduction

- Irish Research: Suggestions for the Beginner
  globalgenealogy.com/globalgazette/gazkb/gazkb33.htm

- Local Ireland
  www.local.ie/genealogy
  Numerous pages; includes messageboard, surname origins, Irish family register, email newsletter etc.

- Shamrock Genealogy
  community-2.webtv.net/shamrockroots

- Tracing your roots in Ireland
  www.shopshamrock.com/genealogy/
  Brief introductory notes with link to bookshop etc.

- When Your Irish Parish Registers Start Too Late
  globalgenealogy.com/globalgazette/gazkb/gazkb35.htm

- What's What in Irish Genealogy Directory Page
  indigo.ie/~gorry/Dir.html
  Basic information, including details of societies, record repositories, events, *etc.*

- Your Irish Roots
  www.youririshroots.com
  Introductory pages

- Seventeenth Century Sources
  freepages.genealogy.rootsweb.com/~irishancestors/Add17.html
  Introduction to *Inquisitions Post Mortem,* Patent Rolls, various muster rolls, tax lists, *etc. etc.*

- Eighteenth Century Sources
  freepages.genealogy.rootsweb.com/~irishancestors/Add18.html
  Covers a wide range of sources

- Nineteenth Century Sources
  freepages.genealogy.rootsweb.com/~irishancestors/Add19.html
  Covers a wide range of sources, including estate records, wills, poor law records, *etc. etc.*

- Guide to Researching Irish Family/Social History in Dundee
  www.fdca.org.uk/irishguide.htm

- Irish Records Index, 1500-1920
  www.ancestry.com/search/rectype/inddbs/4077.htm
  Index to a collection held by the Mormon's Family History Library

3. Libraries, Record Offices and Books

Most of the information sought by genealogists is likely to be found in books and archival sources. The libraries and record offices which hold these resources provide an essential genealogical service, which is unlikely to be replaced by the internet. The value of the latter is in pointing you in the right direction, and helping you to identify the books and records you need to check. Many libraries and record offices now have webpages, listed here. Those which provide internet access to their catalogues are providing a particularly valuable service.

It is impossible here to provide a complete list of library and record office websites likely to be of use to genealogists. Such a list would have to include most public and university libraries, and is outside the scope of this book. However, a number of sites provide extensive listings. Three sites are specifically intended for genealogists:

- Familia: the UK and Ireland's guide to genealogical resources in public libraries
  www.familia.org.uk

- Local Library (Republic of Ireland)
  scripts.ireland.com/ancestor/browse/addresses/librarya__l.htm
  Continued at **/librarym-z.htm**
  List of addresses

- Local Library (Northern Ireland
  scripts.ireland.com/ancestor/browse/addresses/libraryn.htm

There are also a number of general gateways to library sites:
- Consortium of University Research Libraries
  www.curl.ac.uk
  Resources of libraries throughout the British Isles

- Libdex: the Library Index. Ireland
  www.libdex.com/country/Ireland.html

- Libdex: the Library Index. Northern Ireland
  www.libdex.com/country/Northern__Ireland.html

For university library catalogues, consult:
- Irish Academic Library Catalogues
  www.may.ie/library/gateway/other__catalogues.shtml
  List

- Hytelnet: 1st Directory of Internet Resources. Library Catalogs: Ireland
  www.lights.com/hytelnet/ie0/ie000.html
  University Libraries

For a union catalogue of 20 UK and Irish university libraries, consult:
- Copac
  www.copac.ac.uk

For record offices, consult:
- Major Repositories
  scripts.ireland.com/ancestor/browse/addresses/major.htm
  List

- Archon: Historical Manuscripts Commission
  www.hmc.gov.uk/archon/archon.htm
  Includes lists of repositories in Northern Ireland and the Republic of Ireland

- What's What in Irish Genealogy: Record Repositories
  indigo.ie/~gorry/Reposit.html

- Donegal & Northern Ireland Archive Centres
  www.irishancestry.com/archives.htm
  List with brief notes on holdings

See also:
- Historical Manuscripts Commission: Archives in Focus
  www.hmc.gov.uk/focus/focus.htm
  Includes basic information on family history in Northern Ireland.

Major Institutions

British Library
- The British Library
  www.bl.uk
  General Information

- The British Library Public Catalogue
  blpc.bl.uk
  Book catalogue

- British Library Manuscripts Catalogue
  molcat.bl.uk/
  Extensive Irish collection

Family History Library
- Family History Library
  www.familysearch.org
  Library of the Latter Day Saints

- Family History Centres
  www.familysearch.org/eng/Library/FHC/frameset__fhc.asp

- LDS films of interest to those studying Co. Longford families
  personal.nbnet.nb.ca/tmoffatt/ldsfilms.html

- FHC Film and Microfilm
  ahd.exis.net/monaghan/fhc-records.htm
  For Co. Monaghan

Linen Hall Library
- Linen Hall Library, Belfast
  www.linenhall.com
  The leading centre for Irish and local studies in the north of Ireland. Includes catalogue

National Archives of Ireland
- A Guide to the National Archives of Ireland
  homepage.tinet.ie/~seanjmurphy/nai/

- National Archives of Ireland
  www.nationalarchives.ie

- National Archives of Ireland: Genealogy
  www.nationalarchives.ie/genealogy.html

National Library of Ireland
- National Library of Ireland
  www.nli.ie
  Includes catalogue, pages on 'family history research' in the National Library, details of collections, *etc.*

National Archives (UK)
- Irish Genealogy
  www.pro.gov.uk/leaflets/riindex.asp
  Click on title. Resources in the U.K. National Archives

- National Archives
  www.nationalarchives.gov.uk
  (formerly the Public Record Office)

Public Record Office of Northern Ireland
- The Public Record Office of Northern Ireland
  proni.nics.gov.uk/
  Includes page on 'How to trace your family tree', 'understanding the stones' (i.e. monumental inscriptions), and details of the extensive records held

Representative Church Body Library
- Representative Church Body Library
  www.ireland.anglican.org/library/
  Repository of the archives of the Church of Ireland

Ulster American Folk Park
- The Ulster American Folk Park
  www.folkpark.com
  Includes 'The Centre for Migration Studies', with its library and 'emigration database'

University Libraries
- Boole Library, University College Cork, Ireland: Special Collections
  booleweb.ucc.ie/search/subject/speccol/speccol.htm

- University of Dublin. Trinity College
  www.tcd.ie/library

- National University of Ireland, Maynooth
  www.may.ie/library

- University of Ulster Library Services
  www.ulst.ac.uk/library/

Public Libraries

Clare
- Clare Library Local Studies Centre
  www.clarelibrary.ie/eolas/library/local-studies/locstudi1.htm

- Clare County Library
  www.clarelibrary.ie
  Many pages, some listed elsewhere in this directory

Cork
- Cork Archives Institute
  www.corkcorp.ie/facilities/facilities__archive.html

Donegal
- Donegal County Library
  www.donegallibrary.ie/
  Includes pages on 'Donegal Studies' and 'Family History'.

Dublin
- Dublin City Public Libraries
  www.iol.ie/dublincitylibrary/
  Includes the library catalogue, and pages on 'local studies and family history' and 'Dublin City Archives'.

- Sources for the History of Dublin and Ireland
  www.iol.ie/dublincitylibrary/gasources.htm
  In Dublin City Library

- Dun Laoghaire-Rathdown County Council Public Library Service: Local History Department
  www.dlrcoco.ie/library/
  Includes library catalogue, and pages on 'local history'.

- Fingal County Libraries
  www.iol.ie/~fincolib
  Includes pages on 'Local Studies' and 'County Archives'

Galway
- Galway Public Library
  www.galwaylibrary.ie
  Includes page on 'archives' in the local studies dept.

Kerry
- Kerry County Library Local History and Archives Department
  www.kerrycountylibrary.com/
  Click on 'Local History'.

Kildare
- Kildare Heritage & Genealogy Co.
  Kildare.ie/library/KildareHeritage/page2.html

- Genealogical Sources
  Kildare.ie/library/KildareHeritage/page3.html
  At Kildare Heritage and Genealogy Co.

- Kildare Library & Art Services: Kildare Local Studies Department
  kildare.ie/library/localstudies.htm

- Athy Heritage Centre
  kildare.ie/hospitality/historyandheritage/AthyHeritage/index.htm
  Includes list of men from Co. Kildare killed in World War I

Kilkenny
- Kilkenny County Library
  www.familia.org.uk/services/eore/kilkenny.html

Limerick
- Limerick City Public Libraries
  www.limerickcoco.ie/library/local.asp
  Click on 'local studies', 'History', or 'Archives'

Longford
- Longford County Library
  longford.local.ie/content/9837.shtml

Louth
- Louth County Council Services: Archive
  www.louthcoco.ie/louth/html/archive.htm

Mayo
- Library Service for County Mayo
  www.mayo-ireland.ie/Mayo/CoDev/MayoLibs.htm
  Includes pages on 'genealogy' and 'history'

Meath
- Archives and Libraries for Genealogical and Local Historical Research concerning County Meath
  www.angelfire.com/ak2/ashbourne/archives.html

Monaghan
- Monaghan County Council: Library Services
  www.monaghan.ie/library/
  Includes catalogue and a page on genealogy

Roscommon
- Roscommon County Library
  www.iol.ie/~roslib/
  Includes page on 'local history'

Tipperary
- Tipperary Libraries: Local Studies Department
  www.iol.ie/~tipplibs/Local.htm

Waterford
- Waterford City Archives
  www.waterfordcity.ie/archives.htm

Wexford
- Wexford Public Library Services
  www.wexford.ie/Library/
  Includes catalogue with pages on 'Archive Service' and 'Local Studies'

Irish Family History Foundation
This Foundation coordinates a network of government sponsored genealogical research centres which have computerised millions of records. These centres are listed here. The coordinating body is:
- Irish Family History Foundation
  www.irishroots.net

- Report on the Irish Heritage Centre Customer Satisfaction Survey
  tiara.ie/results.htm

For listings of the centres, see:
- County Based Genealogical Centres
  www.nationalarchives.ie/genealogy_countycentres.html

- Local Heritage Centres
  scripts.ireland.com/ancestor/browse/addresses/heritagea-k.htm
  Continued at /heritagel-z.htm

Antrim
- Ulster Historical Foundation
  www.irishroots.net/AntmDown
  Covers Co. Antrim and Co. Down

Armagh
- County Armagh Genealogy: Armagh Ancestry
  www.irish-roots.net/Armagh.htm

Carlow
- Carlow Research Centre
  www.irish-roots.net/Carlow.htm
  www.mayo-ireland.ie/Geneal/Carlow.htm

Clare
- Clare Heritage and Genealogical Centre
  clare.irish-roots.net/

Cork
- Mallow Heritage Centre
  www.irish-roots.net/Cork.htm
  Covers Co. Cork

Donegal
- Donegal Ancestry
  www.irish-roots.net/Donegal.htm

Down
See Antrim

Dublin
- Genealogy in Dublin, Ireland
  www.irish-roots.net/Dublin.htm

Fermanagh
- Irish World
  www.irish-roots.net/FnghTyrn.htm
  Covers Co. Fermanagh and Co. Tyrone

Galway
- Genealogy in Galway in the West of Ireland
  www.irish-roots.net/Galway.htm

Kerry
- Killarney Genealogical Centre
  www.irish-roots.net/Kerry.htm
  Covers Co. Kerry

Kildare
- Kildare Heritage and Genealogy Company
  www.irish-roots.net/Kildare.htm

Kilkenny
- Kilkenny Ancestry
  www.irish-roots.net/Kilknny.htm

Laois
- Laois & Offaly Family History Research Centre
  www.irish-roots.com/LaoisOff.htm

- Irish Midlands Ancestry
  www.irishmidlandsancestry.com
  Covers Laois and Offaly

Leitrim
- Leitrim Genealogy Centre
  www.irish-roots.net/Leitrim.htm

Limerick
- Limerick Ancestry
  www.irishroots.net/Limerick.htm

Londonderry
- County Derry or Londonderry Genealogy Centre
  www.irish-roots.net/Derry.htm

Longford
- Longford Research Centre
  www.irish-roots.net/Longford.htm

Louth
See Meath

Mayo
- Mayo Family History Research Centres
  mayo.irish-roots.net/mayo.htm

Meath
- Meath Heritage Centre
  www.irish-roots.net/Meath.htm

- Meath-Louth Family Research Centre
  www.irish-roots.net/Louth.htm

Monaghan
- Monaghan Research Centre
  www.irish-roots.net/Monaghan.htm

Offaly
See Laois

Roscommon
- County Roscommon Heritage and Genalogy Society
  www.irish-roots.net/Roscmmn.htm

Sligo
- County Sligo Heritage and Genealogy Centre
  www.irish-roots.net/Sligo.htm

Tipperary
- Genealogy in Tipperary
  www.irish-roots.net/Tipp.htm

- Bru Boru Heritage Centre
  www.irishroots.net/STipp.htm
  Covers South Tipperary

- The Tipperary North Family Research Centre
  www.irishroots.net/NTipp.htm

Tyrone
See Fermanagh

Waterford
- Waterford Research Centre
  www.irish-roots.net/Waterford.htm

Westmeath
- Dun na Si Heritage Centre
  www.irish-roots.net/Wstmeath.htm
  Covers Co. Westmeath

Wexford
- Wexford Genealogy Centre
  www.irish-roots.net/Wexford.htm

Wicklow
- Wicklow Research Centre
  www.irish-roots.net/Wicklow.htm

Books

It is vital that the genealogist should be aware of the thousands of published books that may be of assistance in research. They contain far more information than is available on the web. In order to identify them, you need to consult bibliographies. A number are available on the web, and are listed here. Once you have identified the particular books you need, you can find them by checking the library catalogues listed earlier in this chapter.

- Guide to Further Reading
  www.nationalarchives.ie/genealogy4.html

- Sources of Research in Irish Genealogy
  lcweb.loc.gov/rr/genealogy/bib__guid/ireland.html
  Library of Congress bibliography compiled in 1998

- The Irish Ancestral Research Associaton: Books, Publications and Libraries
  tiara.ie/books.html
  Details of books for sale, libraries, publishers, periodicals, etc.

- Northern Irish References: Ulster Province Family History
  www.rootsweb.com/~fianna/NIR/
  Bibliographic guide, with pages on Co's Antrim, Armagh, Donegal, Down, Fermanagh, Londonderry, Monaghan, and Tyrone

Tipperary
- Tipperary Books: a bibliography
  www.rootsweb.com/~irltip2/tipbib.htm
  Brief

Sligo
- County Sligo, Ireland: Books
  www.rootsweb.com/%7Eirlsli/books.html
  Lists books with purchasing details

4. Family History Societies

Many Irish family history societies have websites. These generally provide information on the society - names of officers, meetings, membership information, publications, services offered, lists of members' interests, links to other web pages, *etc.* A number of listings of societies are available:

- Family History and Genealogy Societies: Ireland
  www.genuki.org.uk/Societies/Ireland.html

- Family History Societies
  scripts.ireland.com/ancestor/browse/addresses/family.htm
  Brief list

- Federation of Family History Societies: Irish Societies
  www.ffhs.org.uk/General/Members/Ireland.htm
  Lists addresses

- Irish Genealogical Societies and Periodicals
  globalgenealogy.com/globalgazette/gazkb/gazkb45.htm

For local history societies, see:
- Local History Societies
  scripts.ireland.com/ancestor/browse/addresses/history.htm
  List

National & Regional Organisations
- Council of Irish Genealogical Organisations
  indigo.ie/~gorry/CIGO.html

- Genealogical Society of Ireland
  www.dun-laoghaire.com/genealogy
  welcome.to/GenealogyIreland

- Irish Family History Society
  homepage.eircom.net/~ifhs/

- North of Ireland Family History Society
  www.nifhs.org

- Ulster Historical Foundation
  www.ancestryireland.com

Overseas Societies

Australia

- Australian Institute of Genealogical Studies Inc. Irish Scottish Special Interest Group
  www.aigs.org.au/irscotsig.htm

- Gold Coast and Albert Genealogical Society Inc. Irish Interest Group
  www.winshop.com.au/merv/gcags/irish/

- Irish Ancestry Group: a service group of the Genealogical Society of Victoria
  www.gsv.org.au/irish.htm

- Western Australian Genealogical Society Inc. Special Interest Group. Irish Group
  www.wags.org.au/groups/sigirish.htm

England

- Irish Genealogical Research Society
  www.igrsoc.org/

- Manchester & Lancashire Family History Society: Irish Ancestry Branch
  www.mlfhs.org.uk
  Click on 'Irish Ancestry Branch'

New Zealand

- New Zealand Society of Genealogists Inc. Irish Interest Group
  www.genealogy.org.nz/sig/irish.html

United States

- Irish Genealogical Society Int'l
  www.rootsweb.com/~irish
  Based in Minneapolis area, Minnesota

- American Irish Historical Society
  www.aihs.org

- British Isles Family History Society-U.S.A: Irish Study Group
  www.rootsweb.com/~bifhsusa/study-irish.html

- Irish American Archives Society
  ohioaoh.freeyellow.com/iaas.htm
  Irish emigrants to Cleveland, Ohio

- The Irish Ancestral Research Association
  tiara.ie
  Based in Massachusetts

- Irish Family History Forum
  www.ifhf.org
  Based in New York

- Irish Genealogical Society of Michigan
  www.rootsweb.com/~miigsm/

- Irish Genealogical Society of Wisconsin
  www.execpc.com/~igsw/
  my.execpc.com/~igsw/

- Buffalo Irish Genealogical Society
  www.buffalonet.org/army/bigs.htm

- Irish Palatine Association
  www.local.ie/content/28303.shtml
  For German migrants to Ireland

Local Organisations

Cork

- Cork Genealogical Society
  homepage.tinet.ie/~aocoleman

- Mallow Archaeological & Historical Society
  www.rootsweb.com/~irlmahs/
  For northern Co. Cork

Galway

- East Galway Family History Society
  www.mayo-ireland.ie/Geneal/EtGalway.htm

- West Galway Family History Society
  www.mayo-ireland.ie/Geneal/WtGalway.htm

Offaly

- Offaly Historical & Archaeological Society
  www.offalyhistory.com/index.html

Roscommon

- County Roscommon Family History Society
  www.geocities.com/Heartland/Pines/7030

Tipperary

- Cumann Staire Chontae Thiobraid Arann / County Tipperary Historical Society
  www.iol.ie/~tipplibs/Welcome.htm
  This site is about to be moved

5. Discussion Groups: Mailing Lists and Newsgroups

Want to ask someone who knows? Then join one of the groups listed here. For general information on mailing lists, visit:

- FAQ: Mailing Lists: What are they for?
  helpdesk.rootsweb.com/help/mail1.html

When you join a mailing list, you can send and receive messages from every other member of the group. By way of contrast, you do not have to join the Usenet newsgroups in order to use them; all you need is newsreading software. The two major Irish newsgroups are 'gatewayed' to, and can also be used as, mailing lists. They are:

- **soc.genealogy.ireland**
  Gatewayed to Genire (see below)

- **soc.genealogy.surnames.ireland**
  Gatewayed to IRL-SURNAMES (see below)

An index to the contents of newsgroups is available at:
- Deja's Usenet Archive
  groups.google.com/googlegroups/deja__announcement.html

The most comprehensive listing of mailing lists is:
- Genealogy Resources on the Internet: Ireland mailing lists
  www.rootsweb.com/~jfuller/gen__mail__country-unk-irl.html

See also
- Genealogy Mailing Lists
  www.genuki.org.uk/indexes/MailingLists.html

- The Ireland Gen Web Project: Email lists
  www.irelandgenweb.com/mail.html

- Mailing Lists
  lists.rootsweb.com

General Irish Mailing Lists
- CELTIC QUEST Mailing List
  lists.rootsweb.com/index/intl/IRL/CELTICQUEST.html

- Fianna Mailing List
  lists5.rootsweb.com/index/intl/IRL/FIANNA.html

- Genire Mailing List
  lists5.rootsweb.com/index/intl/IRL/GENIRE.html

- Gen-Trivia Ireland
  lists5.rootsweb.com/index/intl/IRL/GEN-TRIVIA-IRELAND.html

- Ireland Genealogy
  groups.yahoo.com/group/Y-Irl/

- Ireland GenWeb Mailing List
  lists5.rootsweb.com/index/intl/IRL/IrelandGenWeb.html

- Ireland Mailing List
  lists5.rootsweb.com/index/intl/IRL/IRELAND.html

- IRELAND-ROLL-CALLS mailing list
  lists5.rootsweb.com/index/intl/IRL/IRELAND-ROLL-CALLS.html

- Ireland-Roots Mailing List
  lists5.rootsweb.com/index/intl/IRL/IRELAND-ROOTS.html

- irishancestry
  groups.yahoo.com/group/irishancestry

- IrishGenealogy.com
  groups.yahoo.com/group/IrishGenealogy.com
  Newsletter

- IrishGenes Mailing List
  lists5.rootsweb.com/index/intl/IRL/IrishGenes.html

- Shamrock Mailing List
  lists5.rootsweb.com/index/intl/IRL/SHAMROCK.html

Irish Overseas Mailing Lists
- Ethnic-Irish Mailing Lists
  lists.rootsweb.com/index/other/Ethnic__Irish/
  Gateway to 18 lists for the Irish overseas

- Aus-Irish Mailing List
  lists.rootsweb.com/index/other/Ethnic-Irish/AUS-IRISH.html

- Irish Australian
  groups.yahoo.com/group/irishaustralian

- Can-Montreal Mailing List
  lists.rootsweb.com/index/other/Ethnic-Irish/CAN-MONTREAL-IRISH.html

- IRELAND-ROLL-CALLS Mailing List
  lists.rootsweb.com/index/intl/IRL/IRELAND-ROLL-CALLS.html

- Ireland American Lineages and More
  groups.msn.com/IrelandAmericanLineagesandMore/home.htm

- Irish American Obituaries
  lists.rootsweb.com/index/other/Ethnic-Irish/IRISH-AMERICAN-OBITUARIES.html

- OH-Cleveland-Irish Mailing List
  lists.rootsweb.com/index/other/Ethnic-Irish/OH-CLEVELAND-IRISH.html

- IA-Irish Mailing List
  lists.rootsweb.com/index/other/Ethnic-Irish/IA-IRISH.html
  For Irish in Iowa

Specialist Mailing Lists
- Anglo-Irish
  groups.yahoo.com/group/AngloIrish

- Ireland Book-Discussion Mailing List
  lists5.rootsweb.com/index/intl/IRL/IRELAND-BOOK-DISCUSSION.html

- Ireland Cemeteries Mailing List
  lists5.rootsweb.com/index/intl/IRL/IRELAND-CEMETERIES.html

- IRISH-ADOPTEES-SEARCH Mailing List
  lists.rootsweb.com/index/intl/IRL/IRISH-ADOPTEES-SEARCH.html

- IRISH CONVICTS Mailing List
  www.rootsweb.com/index/intl/IRL/IRISH__CONVICTS.html

- IRL-CLANS Mailing List
  lists5.rootsweb.com/index/intl/IRL/IRL-CLANS.html

- IRL-PALATINE Mailing List
  lists5.rootsweb.com/index/intl/IRL/IRL-PALATINE.html

- IRL-TOMBSTONE-INSCRIPTIONS Mailing List
  lists5.rootsweb.com/index/intl/IRL/IRL-TOMBSTONE-INSCRIPTIONS.html

- Irish-Famine Mailing List
  lists5.rootsweb.com/index/intl/IRL/IRISH-FAMINE.html

- FENIANS Mailing List
  lists5.rootsweb.com/index/intl/IRL/FENIANS.html

- Ireland Obits Mailing List
  lists5.rootsweb.com/index/intl/IRL/IRELAND-OBITS.html

- Irish-Adoptees-Search Mailing List
  lists5.rootsweb.com/index/intl/IRL/IRISH-ADOPTEES-SEARCH.html

- IRL-SURNAMES Mailing List
  lists5.rootsweb.com/index/intl/IRL/IRL-SURNAMES.html
  Gatewayed to soc.genealogy.surnames.ireland (see above)

- Scotch-Irish Mailing List
  lists5.rootsweb.com/index/intl/NIR/Scotch-Irish.html

- Transcriptions Eire Mailing List
  lists5.rootsweb.com/index/intl/IRL/TRANSCRIPTIONS-EIRE.html

Provincial Mailing Lists
Connaught
- IRL-CONNAUGHT Mailing List
  lists5.rootsweb.com/index/intl/IRL/IRL-CONNAUGHT.html

Leinster
- IRL-LEINSTER Mailing List
  lists5.rootsweb.com/index/intl/IRL/IRL-LEINSTER.html

Ulster/Northern Ireland
- IRL-Ulster Mailing List
  lists.rootsweb.com/index/intl/NIR/IRL-ULSTER.html

- Northern Ireland Gen Web Mailing List
  lists5.rootsweb.com/index/intl/NIR/NorthernIrelandGenWeb.html

- Northern Ireland Mailing List
  lists5.rootsweb.com/index/intl/NIR/NORTHERN-IRELAND.html

- Northern Ireland Gen Web Mailing List
  lists5.rootsweb.com/index/intl/NIR/NorthernIrelandGenWeb.html

- Unionist-Culture Mailing List
  lists5.rootsweb.com/index/intl/NIR/Unionist-Culture.html
  Covers Northern Ireland

- N-Ireland Mailing List
  lists5.rootsweb.com/index/intl/NIR/N-IRELAND.html

County & Local Mailing Lists

Antrim
- Antrim: a list for the history and genealogy of Co. Antrim
  irishgenealogy.net/mailman/listinfo/antrim__irishgenealogy.net

- IRL-Antrim Mailing List
  lists5.rootsweb.com/index/intl/NIR/IRL-ANTRIM.html

- NIR-Antrim Mailing List
  lists5.rootsweb.com/index/intl/NIR/NIR-ANTRIM.html

- IRL-BELFAST-CITY Mailing List
  lists.rootsweb.com/index/intl/IRL/IRL-BELFAST-CITY.html

Armagh

- NIR-Armagh Mailing List
  lists5.rootsweb.com/index/intl/NIR/NIR-ARMAGH.html

- NIR-Armagh-City Mailing List
  lists5.rootsweb.com/index/intl/NIR/NIR-ARMAGH-CITY.html

Carlow

- IRL-CARLOW Mailing List
  lists5.rootsweb.com/index/intl/IRL/IRL-CARLOW.html

Cavan

- IRL-CAVAN Mailing List
  lists5.rootsweb.com/index/intl/IRL/IRL-CAVAN.html

Clare

- IRL-CLARE Mailing List
  lists5.rootsweb.com/index/intl/IRL/IRL-CLARE.html

Cork

- County Cork Mailing List
  lists5.rootsweb.com/index/intl/IRL/CountyCork.html

- IRL-CORK Mailing List
  lists5.rootsweb.com/index/intl/IRL/IRL-CORK.html

- IRL-CORK-CITY Mailing List
  lists5.rootsweb.com/index/intl/IRL/IRL-CORK-CITY.html

- Beara Mailing List
  lists5.rootsweb.com/index/intl/IRL/Beara.html
  Covers the Berehaven Peninsula, Co's Cork and Kerry

- IRL-CORK-MALLOW Mailing List
  lists.rootsweb.com/index/intl/IRL/IRL-CORK-MALLOW.html

Donegal

- Donegal Mailing List
  www.mindspring.com/~dickod1/donegal/genealogy/maillist__info.htm

- IRL-DONEGAL Mailing List
  lists5.rootsweb.com/index/intl/IRL/IRL-DONEGAL.html

- IRL-CO-DONEGAL Mailing List
  lists5.rootsweb.com/index/intl/IRL/IRL-CO-DONEGAL.html

- IRL-DONEGAL-ROLLCALL Mailing List
  lists5.rootsweb.com/index/intl/IRL/IRL-DONEGAL-ROLLCALL.html

- Donegaleire Mailing List
  lists5.rootsweb.com/index/intl/IRL/DONEGALEIRE.html

- IRL-ARRANMORE Mailing List
  lists5.rootsweb.com/index/intl/IRL/IRL-ARRANMORE.html

Down

- NIR-DOWN Mailing List
  lists5.rootsweb.com/index/intl/NIR/NIR-DOWN.html

Dublin

- IRL-DUBLIN Mailing List
  lists5.rootsweb.com/index/intl/IRL/IRL-DUBLIN.html

- IRL-DUBLIN-CITY Mailing List
  lists5.rootsweb.com/index/intl/IRL/IRL-DUBLIN-CITY.html

Fermanagh

- Fermanagh Gold Mailing List
  lists.rootsweb.com/index/intl/NIR/FERMANAGH-GOLD.html

- Fermanagh Mailing List
  lists5.rootsweb.com/index/intl/NIR/FERMANAGH.html

- IRL-Fermanagh
  lists5.rootsweb.com/index/intl/NIR/IRL-FERMANAGH.html

Galway

- IRL-GALWAY Mailing List
  lists5.rootsweb.com/index/intl/IRL/IRL-GALWAY.html

- IRL-ARAN-ISLANDS Mailing List
  lists5.rootsweb.com/index/intl/IRL/IRL-ARAN-ISLANDS.html

- LETTERMULLEN-GALWAY Mailing List
  lists5.rootsweb.com/index/intl/IRL/LETTERMULLEN-GALWAY.html

- IRL-GALWAY-WOODFORD Mailing List
  lists5.rootsweb.com/index/intl/IRL/IRL-GALWAY-WOODFORD.html

Kerry See also Cork

- IRL-KERRY Mailing List
  lists5.rootsweb.com/index/intl/IRL/IRL-KERRY.html

- IRL-KIL-CASTLECOMER Mailing List
  lists.rootsweb.com/index/intl/IRL/IRL-KIL-CASTLECOMER.html

Kildare

- IRL-CO-KILDARE Mailing Lists
  lists5.rootsweb.com/index/intl/IRL/IRL-CO-KILDARE.html

- IRL-KILDARE Mailing List
  lists5.rootsweb.com/index/intl/IRL/IRL-KILDARE.html

Kilkenny

- IRL-KILKENNY Mailing List
  lists5.rootsweb.com/index/intl/IRL/IRL-KILKENNY.html

- KILKENNY Mailing List
  lists5.rootsweb.com/index/intl/IRL/KILKENNY.html

Laois

- IRL-LAOIS Mailing List
  lists5.rootsweb.com/index/int/IRL/IRL-LAOIS.html

- IRL-LEIX Mailing List
  lists5.rootsweb.com/index/intl/IRL/IRL-LEIX.html

Leitrim

- IRL-LEITRIM Mailing List
  lists5.rootsweb.com/index/intl/IRL/IRL-LEITRIM.html

Limerick

- IRL-LIMERICK Mailing List
  lists5.rootsweb.com/index/intl/IRL/IRL-LIMERICK.html

Londonderry

- NIR-Derry Mailing List
  lists5.rootsweb.com/index/intl/NIR/NIR-DERRY.html

Longford

- IRL-LONGFORD Mailing List
  lists5.rootsweb.com/index/intl/IRL/IRL-LONGFORD.html

Louth

- IRL-LOUTH Mailing List
  lists5.rootsweb.com/index/intl/IRL/IRL-LOUTH.html

Mayo

- IRL-MAYO Mailing List
  lists5.rootsweb.com/index/intl/IRL/IRL-MAYO.html

- MAYO Mailing List
  lists5.rootsweb.com/index/intl/IRL/MAYO.html

- IRL-MAYO-BOHOLA Mailing List
  lists5.rootsweb.com/index/intl/IRL/IRL-MAYO-BOHOLA.html

- IRL-MAYO-CLAREMORRIS Mailing List
  lists5.rootsweb.com/index/intl/IRL/IRL-MAYO-CLAREMORRIS.html

- IRL-MAYO-KILKELLY Mailing List
  lists.rootsweb.com/index/intl/IRL/IRL-MAYO-KILKELLY.html

- IRL-MAYO-KILTIMAGH Mailing List
  lists5.rootsweb.com/index/intl/IRL/IRL-MAYO-KILTIMAGH.html

- IRL-MAYO-KINAFFE-SWINFORD Mailing List
  lists5.rootsweb.com/index/intl/IRL/IRL-MAYO-KINAFFE-SWINFORD.html

- IRL-MAYO-KNOCK Mailing List
  lists.rootsweb.com/index/intl/IRL/IRL-MAYO-KNOCK.html

- IRL-LOUISBURGH mailing list
  lists5.rootsweb.com/index/intl/IRL/IRL-LOUISBURGH.html
  In Co. Mayo

- IRL-MAYO-MIDFIELD Mailing List
  lists.rootsweb.com/index/intl/IRL/IRL-MAYO-MIDFIELD.html

Meath
- IRL-MEATH Mailing List
  lists5.rootsweb.com/index/intl/IRL/IRL-MEATH.html

Monaghan
- IRL-MONAGHAN Mailing List
  lists5.rootsweb.com/index/intl/IRL/IRL-MONAGHAN.html

Munster
- IRL-MUNSTER Mailing List
  lists5.rootsweb.com/index/intl/IRL/IRL-MUNSTER.html

Offaly
- IRL-OFFALY Mailing List
  lists5.rootsweb.com/index/intl/IRL/IRL-OFFALY.html

Roscommon
- IRL-ROSCOMMON Mailing List
  lists5.rootsweb.com/index/intl/IRL/IRL-ROSCOMMON.html

- Roscommon Mailing List
  lists5.rootsweb.com/index/intl/IRL/ROSCOMMON.html

- IRL-BALLYKILCLINE Mailing List
  lists.rootsweb.com/index/intl/IRL/IRL-BALLYKILCLINE.html

Sligo
- IRL-SLIGO Mailing List
  lists5.rootsweb.com/index/intl/IRL/IRL-SLIGO.html

- IRL-BALLYKILCLINE Mailing Lists
  lists5.rootsweb.com/index/intl/IRL/IRL-BALLYKILCLINE.html

Tipperary
- Co. Tipperary Mailing List
  lists5.rootsweb.com/index/intl/IRL/CoTipperary.html

- IRL-TIPPERARY Mailing List
  lists5.rootsweb.com/index/intl/IRL/IRL-TIPPERARY.html

Tyrone
- Co. Tyrone, Ireland, Mailing List
  lists5.rootsweb.com/index/intl/NIR/CoTyroneIreland.html

- IRL-TYRONE Mailing List
  lists5.rootsweb.com/index/intl/NIR/IRL-TYRONE.html

- NIR-Tyrone Mailing List
  lists5.rootsweb.com/index/intl/NIR/NIR-TYRONE.html

Waterford
- IRL-WATERFORD Mailing List
  lists5.rootsweb.com/index/intl/IRL/IRL-WATERFORD.html

- Waterford Mailing List
  lists5.rootsweb.com/index/intl/IRL/WATERFORD.html

Westmeath
- IRL-WESTMEATH Mailing List
  lists5.rootsweb.com/index/intl/IRL/IRL-WESTMEATH.html

Wexford
- IRL-WEXFORD Mailing List
  lists5.rootsweb.com/index/intl/IRL/IRL-WEXFORD.html

- Wexford Mailing List
  lists5.rootsweb.com/index/intl/IRL/WEXFORD.html

- IRL-WEX-ENNISCORTHY Mailing List
  lists.rootsweb.com/index/intl/IRL/IRL-WEX-ENNISCORTHY.html

Wicklow
- IRL-WICKLOW Mailing List
  lists5.rootsweb.com/index/intl/IRL/IRL-WICKLOW.html

6. Message/Query Boards

A number of websites offer you the opportunity to post messages / queries on the site itself. For a listing of such sites visit:

- Queries and Message Boards
  www.CyndisList.com/queries.htm

A number of sites offer boards for every Irish county. These include:
- Genforum: Ireland: Regions
  genforum.genealogy.com/ireland/regions.html
  Boards for every Irish county

- Ireland GenWeb Project: Query Message Boards
  www.irelandgenweb.com/query.html
  Boards for 'Ireland' and 'Northern Ireland'

- Rootsweb.com: [Message Boards]: Ireland
  boards.ancestry.com
  Click on 'United Kingdom and Ireland', and on 'Ireland'. Boards for every Irish county

See also:
- CAORA
  www.caora.net/
  Collection of message boards for every county, *etc.*

- Virtual Irish Community
  www.vic.ie

General Message Boards
- The Information About Ireland Site Genealogy Forum
  www.ireland-information.com/board/wwwboard.html

- Ireland Genealogy Forum
  genforum.genealogy.com/ireland/

- Ireland Genealogy Message Board
  www.voy.com/43747/

- Irish Emigrant Message Board
  www.theirishemigrant.com/Board/default.asp

- Irish Ancestral Pages
  groups.msn.com/IrishAncestralPages

- Scottish and Irish Genealogy Forum
  pub30.bravenet.com/forum/showasp?usernum=2518170574

- Irish Genealogy
  www.myirishancestry.com
  Click on 'message board and forum'

County Boards

These are in addition to the major collections of county boards listed above.

Carlow

- Carlow Ireland Queries
  genconnect.rootsweb.com/gc/Ireland/Carlow

Donegal

- Donegal, Ireland Connection Boards
  freepages.genealogy.rootsweb.com/~donegaleire/Donconnect.html
  List of bulletin boards, *etc.*

- Carndonagh/Inishowen Message Board
  users2.cgiforme.com/carn/cfmboard.html

Down

- County Down Ireland Queries
  genconnect.rootsweb.com/gc/Ireland/Down

Fermanagh

- Fermanagh Forum
  www.fermanagh.org.uk/forum.htm

Galway

- Galway County Ireland Queries
  www.rootsweb.com/~irlgal/index2.html

Leitrim

- The Leitrim-Roscommon Genealogy Bulletin Board
  www.leitrim-roscommon.com/lrboard/

Mayo

- Mayo International Ltd: Bulletin Boards
  mail.mayo-ireland.ie/Webx

Roscommon

See Leitrim

Tyrone

- County Tyrone Query
  www.rootsweb.com/~nirtyr3/Queries.htm

Waterford

- Knowhere Noticeboard for Waterford
  www.knowhere.co.uk/board/kb490/

7. County Pages

A great deal of information is to be found on county pages. A number of private individuals have created their own county pages, but four organisations have provided pages for every Irish county. The *Irish Times* sites provide the most useful introductory information, but have few links. *Genuki* concentrates attention on primary historical information, rather than on-going and completed research. *Genweb* has some similar information but also includes query boards for each county, and has more information on current and completed research. *Fianna* sites offer a wide range of general information on resources, with many links. *From Ireland* county sites include information under standard headings such as 'gravestones', 'journals', 'religious records', 'links', *etc.*

For a listing of county websites on Rootsweb, see:
- Ireland and Northern Ireland
  www.rootsweb.com/~websites/international/uk.html#ireland

For Northern Ireland, see:
- Genealogy Planet: Northern Ireland Genealogy & Regional Resources
  www.genealogytoday.com/genealogy/planet/earth/europe.html
  Click on 'Ireland', and also on 'United Kingdom' (for Northern Ireland).
  Gateway

- The Northern Ireland Online Genealogy Centre
  www.nireland.com/genealogy
  Introductory pages

- Northern Ireland Research: Selected Resources
  globalgenealogy.com/globalgazette/gazkb/gazkb60.htm

- The Province of Ulster
  scripts.ireland.com/ancestor/browse/counties/ulster/

Antrim
- Antrim: From Ireland
  www.from-ireland.net/contents/antrimcont.htm

- County Antrim: Fianna's County Page
  www.rootsweb.com/~fianna/county/antrim.html

- Co. Antrim GenWeb
  www.rootsweb.com/~nirantri/

- County Antrim, Ireland: Ireland Genealogical Projects
  www.rootsweb.com/~nirant/Antrim/
  www.geocities.com/Heartland/Flats/4612/antrim.html

- Genuki Co. Antrim
  www.genuki.org.uk/big/irl/ANT/

- County Antrim, Ireland
  www.rootsweb.com/~nirant/Antrim/

- Co. Antrim's Web Page
  genealogy.port5.com/

- Irish Ancestors: County Antrim
  scripts.ireland.com/ancestor/browse/counties/ulster/index__an.htm

Armagh
- Armagh: From Ireland
  www.from-ireland.net/contents/armaghconts.htm

- Co. Armagh: Ireland Genealogy Projects
  www.rootsweb.com/~nirarm2

- County Armagh: Fianna County Page
  www.rootsweb.com/~fianna/county/armagh.html
  Addresses and links

- Genuki Co. Armagh
  www.genuki.org.uk/big/irl/ARM/

- County Armagh: Irish Times
  scripts.ireland.com/ancestor/browse/counties/ulster/index__ar.htm

Carlow
- Carlow County I.G.P.
  www.rootsweb.com/~irlcar2/

- Carlow: From Ireland
  www.from-ireland.net/contents/carlcont.htm

- County Carlow Gen Web
  www.rootsweb.com/~irlcar/

- Genuki Co. Carlow
  www.genuki.org.uk/big/irl/CAR/

- County Carlow: Irish Times
  scripts.ireland.com/ancestor/browse/counties/leinster/index__ca.htm

Cavan
- Cavan: From Ireland
  www.from-ireland.net/contents/cavancont.htm

- County Cavan
  www.rootsweb.com/~fianna/county/cavan.html

- Co. Cavan Gen Web
  www.irelandgenweb.com/cavan.html

- Co. Cavan, Ireland, Research Site
  freepages.genealogy.rootsweb.com/~adrian/Cavan.htm

- Genuki Co. Cavan
  www.genuki.org/big/irl/CAV

- County Cavan. Irish Times
  scripts.ireland.com/ancestor/browse/counties/ulster/index__ca.htm

- Al Beagan's Genealogy Notes of Co. Cavan
  members.tripod.com/~Al__Beagan/tcavan.htm
  Includes many notes on parishes.

Clare
- Clare: From Ireland
  www.from-ireland.net/contents/clareconts.htm

- County Clare
  www.rootsweb.com/~irlcla/

- County Clare: Fianna County Page
  www.rootsweb.com/~fianna/county/clare.html

- County Clare Gen Web
  www.rootsweb.com/~irlcla2/

- Genuki Co. Clare
  home.pacbell.net/nymets11/genuki/CLA/

- County Clare, Ireland
  www.connorsgenealogy.com/clare

- County Clare: Irish Times
  scripts.ireland.com/ancestor/browse/counties/munster/index__cl.htm

See also Limerick

Cork
- Cork
  freepages.genealogy.rootsweb.com/~nyirish/CORK%20Index
  Includes extracts from various sources

- Cork Ancestors
  homepage.eircom.net/~ridgway/
  Collection of trade directories, newspaper extracts, electoral records, *etc.*

- County Cork
  www.sci.net.au/userpages/mgrogan/cork/ire.cork.htm
  Gateway to Co. Cork sites on Rootsweb

- County Cork: Fianna County Page
  www.rootsweb.com/~fianna/county/cork.html

- County Cork Gen Web
  www.rootsweb.com/~irlcor

- Genuki Co. Cork
  www.genuki.org.uk/big/irl/COR/

- County Cork: Irish Times
  scripts.ireland.com/ancestor/browse/counties/munster/index__co.htm

- Ginni Swanton's Web Site
  www.ginnisw.com/
  Includes transcripts and indexes etc. of many sources for Co. Cork

Donegal

- County Donegal: Fianna County Page
  www.rootsweb.com/~fianna/county/donegal.htm

- Co. Donegal Gen Web
  www.rootsweb.com/~irldon

- Donegal. From Ireland
  www.from-ireland.net/contents/donegalconts.htm

- Genuki Co. Donegal
  www.genuki.org.uk/big/irl/DON/

- County Donegal: Irish Times
  scripts.ireland.com/ancestor/browse/counties/ulster/index__do.htm

- Donegal: I.G.P.
  www.mindspring.com/dickod1/donegal/

- Donegal, Ireland
  freepages.genealogy.rootsweb.com/~donegaleire/Doncontent.html

- Donegal Resources held by the L.D.S.
  freepages.genealogy.rootsweb.com/~donegal/ldsrec.htm

- S. W. Donegal Irish Genealogy & our Irish Heritage
  www.radiks.net/~keving/Donegal/DonegalGen.html
  County page; includes much bibliographic information.

Down

- County Down: Ireland Genealogy Projects
  www.rootsweb.com/~nirdow2/

- Down: From Ireland
  www.from-ireland.net/contents/downconts.htm

- County Down: Fianna County Page
  www.rootsweb.com/~fianna/county/down.html

- Co. Down Gen Web
  www.rootsweb.com/~nirdow/

- Genuki Co. Down
  www.genuki.org.uk/big/irl/DOW/

- County Down: Irish Times
  scripts.ireland.com/ancestor/browse/counties/ulster/index__dn.htm

- The Down, Ireland, Genealogy Web Site
  www.caora.net
  Searchable databases of the Flax Grants (1796), Tithe Record (1820-1830's), Griffiths Valuation (1863), and Census summaries (1901); also message board, chat room, etc.

- Raymonds County Down Website
  www.raymondscountydownwebsite.com/

Dublin

- Dublin: From Ireland
  www.from-ireland.net/contents/dublincontents.htm

- County Dublin: Fianna County Page
  www.rootsweb.com/~fianna/county/dublin.html

- Co. Dublin Gen Web
  www.rootsweb.com/~irldub.

- County Dublin, Ireland: Ireland Genealogical Projects
  www.rootsweb.com/~irldubli/

- Genuki Co. Dublin
  www.genuki.org.uk/big/irl/DUB/

- County Dublin: Irish Times
  scripts.ireland.com/ancestor/browse/counties/leinster/index__du.htm

Fermanagh

- County Fermanagh: Fianna County Page
  www.rootsweb.com/~fianna/county/fermanagh.html

- Co. Fermanagh
  www.rootsweb.com/~nirfer/

- County Fermanagh: Irish Times
  scripts.ireland.com/ancestor/browse/counties/ulster/index__fe.htm

- Fermanagh: From Ireland
  www.from-ireland.net/contents/fermanconts.htm

- Fermanagh: Ireland Genealogy Projects
  www.rootsweb.com/~nirfer2/

- Fermanagh Presents
  www.fermanagh.org.uk/fermanaghpresents/

- Fermanagh Gold
  www.fermanagh.org.uk

- Genuki Co. Fermanagh
  www.genuki.org.uk/big/irl/FER/

Galway

- Galway
  freepages.genealogy.rootsweb.com/~nyirish/GALWAY%20index
  Includes many extracts from various sources

- Galway: From Ireland
  www.from-ireland.net/contents/galwayconts.htm

- County Galway: Fianna County Page
  www.rootsweb.com/~fianna/county/galway.html

- Co. Galway Gen Web
  www.rootsweb.com/~irlgal/Galway.html

- County Galway: Ireland Genealogy Projects
  www.rootsweb.com/~irlgal2

- Genuki Co. Galway
  www.genuki.org.uk/big/irl/GAL/

- County Galway: Irish Times
  scripts.ireland.com/ancestor/browse/counties/connacht/index__ga.htm

Kerry

See also Clare

- Kerry: From Ireland
  www.from-ireland.net/contents/kerrycontents.htm

- County Kerry: Fianna County Page
  www.rootsweb.com/~fianna/county/kerry.html

- Co. Kerry Gen Web
  www.rootsweb.com/~irlker

- Genuki Co. Kerry
  www.genuki.org.uk/big/irl/KER/

- County Kerry: Irish Times
  scripts.ireland.com/ancestor/browse/counties/munster/index__ke.htm

- Finding your Ancestors in Kerry
  www.rootsweb.com/~irlker/find.html
  Introduction

- A Dingle, Co. Kerry, Ireland Genealogical Helper
  members.aol.com/waterlilys/

Kildare

- County Kildare: Fianna County Page
  www.rootsweb.com/~fianna/county/kildare.htm

- Co. Kildare, Ireland: Ireland Genealogy Projects
  www.rootsweb.com/~irlkid

- Genuki Co. Kildare
  www.genuki.org.uk/big/irl/KID/

- County Kildare: Irish Times
  scripts.ireland.com/ancestry/browse/counties/leinster/index__ke.htm

- Kildare: From Ireland
  www.from-ireland.net/contents/kilcont.htm

Kilkenny

- County Kilkenny: Fianna County Page
  www.rootsweb.com/~fianna/county/kilkenny.html

- Co. Kilkenny Gen Web
  www.rootsweb.com/~irlkik

- County Kilkenny Genealogy: Ireland Genealogy Projects
  www.rootsweb.com/~irlkik2/

- Genuki Co. Kilkenny
  www.genuki.org.uk/big/irl/KIK/

- County Kilkenny: Irish Times
  scripts.ireland.com/ancestor/browse/counties/leinster/index__ki.htm

- Kilkenny. From Ireland
  www.from-ireland.net/contents/kilkenconts.htm

Laois

- County Laois (Queen's, Leix)
  www.rootsweb.com/~fianna/county/laois.html

- The Genealogy of County Laois (Queen's) Ireland: I.G.P.
  www.rootsweb.com/~irllex

- Laois (Queen's County) Gen Web
  www.rootsweb.com/~irllao

- Genuki Co. Laois (Queen's)
  www.genuki.org.uk/big/irl/LEX

- County Laois: Irish Times
  scripts.ireland.com/ancestor/browse/counties/leinster/index__la.htm

- Laois (Leix, Queen's County): From Ireland
  www.from-ireland.net/contents/laoisconts.htm

Leitrim

- Leitrim: From Ireland
  www.from-ireland.net/contents/leitrimconts.htm

- County Leitrim: Fianna County Page
  www.rootsweb.com/~fianna/county/leitrim.html

- Co. Leitrim Gen Web
  www.irelandgenweb.com/~leitrim

- County Leitrim: Leitrim Genweb
  www.rootsweb.com/~irllet/

- Genuki Co. Leitrim
  www.genuki.org.uk/big/irl/LET

- County Leitrim: Irish Times
  scripts.ireland.com/ancestor/browse/counties/connacht/index__le.htm
- Leitrim-Roscommon Genealogy Web Site
  www.leitrim-roscommon.com/

Limerick
- County Limerick, Ireland
  www.connorsgenealogy.com/LIM/index.htm
- County Limerick: Fianna County Page
  www.rootsweb.com/~fianna/county/limerick.html
- County Limerick Genealogy
  www.rootsweb.com/~irllim/
- Genuki Co. Limerick
  home.pacbell.net/nymets11/genuki/LIM/
- County Limerick: Irish Times
  scripts.ireland.com/ancestor/browse/counties/munster/index__li.htm
- County Limerick Genealogy
  www.geocities.com/jackreidy/limerick.htm
  www.geocities.com/Athens/Parthenon/6108/limerick.htm
  Genweb site
- Limerick: From Ireland
  www.from-ireland.net/contents/limerickconts.htm
- McNamara & McCarthy
  home.att.net/~wexlababe
  Many pages relating to Limerick, Clare, and Kerry

Londonderry
- County Londonderry: Fianna County Page
  www.rootsweb.com/~fianna/county/derry.html
- Co. Londonderry Gen Web
  www.rootsweb.com/~nirldy
- Londonderry (Derry): From Ireland
  www.from-ireland.net/contents/londderryconts.htm
- County Londonderry, Northern Ireland: Ireland Genealogy Projects
  www.rootsweb.com/~nirldy2/
- Genuki Co. Londonderry
  www.genuki.org.uk/big/irl/LDY/
- County Derry: Irish Times
  scripts.ireland.com/ancestor/browse/counties/ulster/index__de.htm

See also Leitrim

Longford
- County Longford: Fianna County Page
  www.rootsweb.com/~fianna/county/longford.html
- The Genealogy of County Longford, Ireland
  www.rootsweb.com/~irllog
  I.G.P. site
- Genuki Co. Longford
  www.skylinc.net/~las2002/genuki/LOG/
- Longford: From Ireland
  www.from-ireland.net/contents/longforconts.htm
- Longford Genealogy
  longford.local.ie/genealogy
- Edgeworthstown Parish Scrapbook
  www.mostrim.org/Scrapbook/
  Includes various lists, e.g. famine victims 1847

Louth

- County Louth: Fianna's County Page
  www.rootsweb.com/~fianna/county/louth.html

- County Louth, Ireland: Ireland Genealogy Projects
  www.rootsweb.com/~irllou/

- County Louth, Ireland, Genealogical Sources
  www.jbhall.freeservers.com
  Includes many name lists

- Genuki Co. Louth
  www.genuki.org.uk/big/irl/LOU

- Louth: From Ireland
  www.from-ireland.net/contents/louthcontents.htm

Mayo

- County Mayo: Fianna County Page
  www.rootsweb.com/~fianna/county/mayo.html

- County Mayo: Ireland Genealogy Projects
  www.rootsweb.com/~irlmay/

- County Mayo, Ireland
  www.connorsgenealogy.com/mayo/
  Little information at date of publication, but the site is 'under construction'

- Genuki Co. Mayo
  www.genuki.org.uk/big/irl/MAY/

- County Mayo: Irish Times
  scripts.ireland.com/ancestor/browse/counties/connacht/index__ma.htm

- Co. Mayo, Ireland, Genealogy
  www.geocities.com/Heartland/Acres/4031/mayo.html

- Mayo: From Ireland
  www.from-ireland.net/contents/mayoconts.htm

Meath

See also Leitrim

- Co. Meath: Irish Times
  scripts.ireland.com/ancestor/browse/counties/leinster/index__me.htm

- County Meath Fianna County Page
  www.rootsweb.com/~fianna/county/meath.html

- County Meath, Republic of Ireland: Ireland Genealogy Projects
  www.rootsweb.com/~irlmea/

- Genuki Co. Meath
  www.genuki.org.uk/big/irl/MEA

- Ireland Genealogy Projects: County Meath
  www.rootsweb.com/~irlmea2/

- Meath: From Ireland
  www.from-ireland.net/contents/meathconts.htm

- Meath: Ireland Gen Web
  hometown.aol.com/mathewsb01/meath/meath.htm

Monaghan

- County Monaghan: Fianna's County Page
  www.rootsweb.com/~fianna/county/monaghan.html

- Co. Monaghan Genealogy
  www.rootsweb.com/~irlmog2/

- County Monaghan: Ireland Genealogy Projects
  www.rootsweb.com/~irlmog/

- Genuki Co. Monaghan
  www.genuki.org.uk/big/irl/MOG/

- County Monaghan: Irish Times
  scripts.ireland.com/ancestor/browse/counties/ulster/index__mo.htm

- Monaghan: From Ireland
  www.from-ireland.net/contents/monaghanconts.htm

- Monaghan: the County
  www.exis.net/ahd/monaghan/default.htm
  ahd.exis.net/monaghan/

Offaly

- County Offaly (King's): Fianna County Page
  www.rootsweb.com/~fianna/county/offaly.html

- Co. Offaly (King's County) Gen Web
  www.irelandgenweb.com/offaly.html

- Genuki Co. Offaly (King's Co.)
  www.genuki.org.uk/big/irl/OFF/

- County Offaly: Irish Times
  scripts.ireland.com/ancestor/browse/counties/leinster/index__of.htm

- Offaly (King's County)
  www.from-ireland.net/contents/offalyconts.htm

- Offaly, Ireland: King's County
  www.geocities.com/Heartland/Flats/4612/offaly.html

Roscommon

- The County Roscommon Database
  www.rootsweb.com/~irlros/

- County Roscommon: Fianna County Page
  www.rootsweb.com/~fianna/county/roscommon.html

- Co. Roscommon Gen Web
  www.rootsweb.com/~irlrosco/

- Genuki Co. Roscommon
  www.genuki.org.uk/big/irl/ROS

- County Roscommon: Irish Times
  scripts.ireland.com/ancestor/browse/counties/connacht/index__ro.htm

- Roscommon: From Ireland
  www.from-ireland.net/contents/roscommconts.htm

Sligo

- County Sligo: Fianna County Page
  www.rootsweb.com/~fianna/county/sligo.html

- Co. Sligo Gen Web
  www.rootsweb.com/~irlsli

- County Sligo, Ireland: Ireland Genealogy Projects
  www.rootsweb.com/~irlsli2/

- Genuki Co. Sligo
  www.genuki.org.uk/big/irl/SLI

- County Sligo: Irish Times
  scripts.ireland.com/ancestor/browse/counties/connaught/index__sl.htm

- Sligo: From Ireland
  www.from-ireland.net/contents/sligoconts

Tipperary

- County Tipperary: Fianna County Page
  www.rootsweb.com/~fianna/county/tipperary.html

- Co. Tipperary Gen Web
  www.rootsweb.com/~irltip/tipperary.htm

- County Tipperary, Ireland
  www.connorsgenealogy.com/tipp/

- County Tipperary, Ireland Genealogy
  www.rootsweb.com/~irltip2/

- Genuki Co. Tipperary
  home.carolina.rr.com/ninah/genuki/TIP/

- County Tipperary: Irish Times
  scripts.ireland.com/ancestor/browse/counties/munster/index__ti.htm

- Tipperary: From Ireland
  www.from-ireland.net/contents/tipperconts.htm

- Tipperary, Ireland: Genealogies & Cemeteries
  www.geocities.com/luanndevries/
  Collection of sources, extracts and indexes

- Genealogical Research: Clogheen & District
  www.iol.ie/~clogheen/
  Introduction to parish sources

Tyrone
- County Tyrone: Fianna's County Page
  www.rootsweb.com/~Fianna/county/tyrone.html

- Co. Tyrone Gen Web
  www.rootsweb.com/~nirtyr

- Co. Tyrone Genealogy
  freepages.genealogy.rootsweb.com/~tyrone/

- Genuki Co. Tyrone
  www.genuki.org.uk/big/irl/TYR/

- County Tyrone: Irish Times
  scripts.ireland.com/ancestor/browse/counties/ulster/index__ty.htm

- Tyrone: From Ireland
  www.from-ireland.net/contents/tyroneconts.htm

- Tyrone: Ireland Genealogy Projects
  www.rootsweb.com/~nirtyr3/

Waterford
- County Waterford: Fianna's County Page
  www.rootsweb.com/~fianna/county/waterford.html

- County Waterford Genealogy
  www.rootsweb.com/~irlwat2/

- County Waterford: Irish Times
  scripts.ireland.com/ancestor/browse/counties/munster/index__wa.htm

- Genuki Co. Waterford
  www.genuki.org.uk/big/irl/WAT

- Waterford County: [Gen Web]
  community2-webtv.net/@HH!0A!26!88E51C93F97C/
  waterfordroots/waterford

- Waterford: From Ireland
  www.from-ireland.net/contents/waterfordconts.htm

Westmeath
- County Westmeath: Fianna's County Page
  www.rootsweb.com/~fianna/county/westmeath.html

- County Westmeath of Ireland: Ireland Genealogy Projects
  www.rootsweb.com/~irlwem2/

- Genuki Co. Westmeath
  www.genuki.org.uk/big/irl/WEM

- Westmeath: From Ireland
  www.from-ireland.net/contents/westmeathconts.htm

- Westmeath Gen Web
  www.rootsweb.com/~irlwem

- County Westmeath: Irish Times
  scripts.ireland.com/ancestor/browse.counties/leinster/index__we.htm

Wexford
- County Wexford: Fianna's County Page
  www.rootsweb.com/~fianna/county/wexford.html

- Genuki Co. Wexford
  www.genuki.org.uk/big/irl/WEX/

- Ireland, Gen Web: Co. Wexford
  www.rootsweb.com/~irlwex

- County Wexford: Irish Times
  scripts.ireland.com/ancestor/browse/counties/leinster/index__wd.htm

- Ireland, County Wexford: Ireland Genealogy Projects
  users.rootsweb.com/~irlwex2/

- Wexford
  freepages.genealogy.rootsweb.com/~nyirish/
  WEXFORD%20%20Index.html
  Includes extracts from various sources

- Wexford: From Ireland
  www.from-ireland.net/wexfordconts.htm

Wicklow
- County Wicklow: Fianna's County Page
  www.rootsweb.com/~fianna/county/wicklow.html

- Co. Wicklow [Gen Web]
  www.rootsweb.com/~irlwic/

- County Wickow Genealogy
  www.rootsweb.com/~irlwic2/

- County Wicklow: Irish Times
  scripts.ireland.com/ancestor/browse/counties/leinster/index__wi.htm

- Genuki Co. Wicklow
  www.genuki.org.uk/big/irl/WIC/

- Wicklow: From Ireland
  www.from-ireland.net/contents/wicklowconts.htm

8. Surnames

The Internet is an invaluable aid for those who want to make contact with others researching the same surname. There are innumerable lists of surname interests, family web-sites, and surname mailing lists. The two latter categories will not be listed here; they are far too numerous for a book of this length, and many are international in scope rather than purely Irish. Such sites may be found through the gateways listed below.

For general guidance on finding surname information on the web, consult:

- Finding Surname Interests
  www.hawgood.co.uk/finding.htm
  General discussion of surnames on the web.

See also:
- Researching Irish Names
  www.rootsweb.com/~fianna/surname/
  General guidance on using surname lists with many links.

Surname Web Pages
Surname web-pages are listed in the following pages:
- A-Z of Ireland Family Surnames Page
  members.tripod.com/~Caryl__Williams/Eirenames-7.html

- Personal Home Pages
  www.CyndisList.com/personal.htm
  Good starting point, but with American bias.

- Cyndis List: Surname, Family Association & Family newsletters index
  www.cyndislist.com/surnames.htm
  American bias

- Irish Clans & Families
  www.scotlandsclans.com/irclans.htm
  Directory of family pages

- Irish Surname Pages
  www.geocities.com/jackreidy/surnames.htm

- Irish Surnames and Irish Descendants Homepages
  www.geocities.com/Heartland/Meadows/4404/pages.html
  Brief gateway

- Links to Irish Names
  www.rootsweb.com/~fianna/surname/name02.html
  Surname webpage directory

- Roots Web Surname List
  qrsl.rootsweb.com/cgi-bin/rslsql.cgi
  International, but with many Irish names

- Surname Helper Home Page
  surhelp.rootsweb.com
  Gateway

- Surname Helper Ireland
  surhelp-bin.rootsweb.com/sitelist.pl
  Lists (mainly) Irish Gen Web sites

- Surname Websites [at Rootsweb]
  www.rootsweb.com/~websites/surnames/
  Scroll down; probably the most extensive listing of surname sites; American bias

- Surname Resources at Rootsweb
  resources.rootsweb.com/~clusters/surnames/

The major on-line surname interests listing for Ireland is:
- On-line Irish Names Research Directory
  www.users.on.net/proformat/irlnames.html
  Extensive interest lists, by county

See also:
- Curious Fox: Ireland
  www.curiousfox.com/uk/ireland.lasso

- Genealogical Research Directory
  www.ozemail.com.au/-grdxxx
  Webpage for the major published interests listing, available as a book or CD

- Genuki Surname Lists
  www.genuki.org.uk/indexes/SurnamesLists.html
  Interests

- The Irish Ancestral Research Association: Members Surname Interests
  tiara.ie/surnames.htm

- Irish Family Surname Interest List
  irishgenealogy.net/surnamef.html

- The Ulster Genealogical Database
  uhp.future.easyspace.com/genealogy/
  Surname interests

A variety of databases can be searched for surnames at:
- Surname Navigator Ireland
  www.rat.de/kuijsten/navigator/ireland/

County and Local Surname Websites

Antrim
- Co. Antrim A-Z
  www.users.on.net/proformat/antnames1.html

- Co. Antrim Families on the Web
  www.geocities.com/Heartland/Prairie/4592/antlink.html
  Directory of web pages

- Co. Antrim Family Surname & Irish Family Surname Interest List
  irishgenealogy.net/antrimgen.html#SURNAME

- The Antrim County Surname List
  www.ole.net/~maggie/antrim/surnames.htm

Armagh
- Armagh A-Z
  www.users.on.net/proformat/armnames1.html

Carlow
- Co. Carlow A-Z
  www.users.on.net/proformat/carnames1.html

- County Carlow Surname Registry
  www.rootsweb.com/~irlcar2/registry.htm

Cavan
- Co. Cavan A-Z
  www.users.on.net/proformat/cavnames1.html

Clare
- Co. Clare A-Z
  www.users.on.net/proformat/clanames1.html
  Surname interests. Continued by **/clanames2.html**

Cork
- Co. Cork A-Z
  www.users.on.net/proformat/cornames1.html

- Ginni Swanton's Web Site: County Cork Surnames Database
  www.ginnisw.com/Surnames%20Home.htm

Donegal
- Co. Donegal A-Z
  www.users.on.net/proformat/donnames1.html

- County Donegal Surname Researchers
  www.geocities.com/Heartland/Estates/6587/Donresearch.html
  Web pages

- Co. Donegal People Locator
  www.donfam.50megs.com/page12.htm
  Surnames index to sources

Down
- Co. Down A-Z
  www.users.on.net/proformat/downames1.html

Dublin
- Co. Dublin A-Z
  www.users.on.net/proformat/dubnames1.html

Fermanagh
- Co. Fermanagh A-Z
  www.users.on.net/proformat/fernames1.html

- Surnames on Fermanagh Gold
  www.fermanagh.org.uk/genealogy/allnames.htm

Galway
- County Galway Surname List
  www.labyrinth.net.au/~quibellg/galway.htm

Kerry
- Family Association Websites
  www.rootsweb.com/~irlker/familywebs.html
  For Co. Kerry

- Co. Kerry A-Z
  www.users.on.net/proformat/kernames1.html

Kildare
- Co. Kildare A-Z
  www.users.on.net/proformat/kidnames1.html

Kilkenny
- County Kilkenny. Surnames
  www.rootsweb.com/irlkik2/
  Click on 'Surnames'

- County Kilkenny, Ireland, Genealogy: Surnames of Kilkenny
  www.rootsweb.com/~irlkik/ksurname.htm#sons
  Gateway to surname pages, coats of arms, etc.

Laois
- Co. Leix A-Z
  www.users.on.net/proformat/lexnames1.html

Leitrim
- Leitrim-Roscommon Surname Search Page
  www.leitrim-roscommon.com/surname__intro.html

Limerick
- County Limerick Surname Roster
  www.connorsgenealogy.com/LIM/
  Click on title

Londonderry
- Derry A-Z
  www.users.on.net/proformat/ldynames1.html

- Londonderry Surname Queries
  www.thauvin.net/chance/ireland/derry/queries.jsp

Longford
- Co. Longford A-Z
  www.users.on.net/proformat/lognames1.html

- Longford Surnames Online
  www.rootsweb.com/~irllog/longford.htm

Louth
- Co. Louth A-Z
  www.users.on.net/proformat/lounames1.html

Mayo
- The County Mayo Surname Interest List
  www.cs.ncl.ac.uk/genuki/SurnamesList/MAY.html

- Mayo A-Z
  www.users.on.net/proformat/maynames1.html

Meath
- Co. Meath A-Z
  www.users.on.net/proformat/meanames1.html

Monaghan
- Co. Monaghan A-Z
  www.users.on.net/proformat/mognames1.html

Offaly
- Co. Offaly A-Z
  www.users.on.net/proformat/offnames1.html

Roscommon
See Leitrim

Sligo
- Co. Sligo A-Z
  www.users.on.net/proformat/slinames1.html

Tipperary
- County Tipperary Surname Registry
  www.rootsweb.com/~irltip2/
  Interests

- The Tipperary Surnames List
  homepages.ihug.co.nz/~hughw/tip.html

Tyrone
- Co. Tyrone A-Z
  www.users.on.net/proformat/tyrnames1.html

Waterford
- County Waterford Surname Registry
  www.rootsweb.com/~irlwat2/registry.htm

- Co. Waterford A-Z
  www.users.on.net/proformat/watnames1.html

Westmeath
- Co. Westmeath A-Z
  www.users.on.net/proformat/wemnames1.html

- County Westmeath Surname Registry
  www.rootsweb.com/~irlwem2/registry.htm
  Interests

Wexford
- Co. Wexford A-Z
  www.users.on.net/proformat/wexnames1.html

- The Wexford Surnames List
  homepages.ihug.co.nz/~hughw/wexford.html

Wicklow
- Co. Wick A-Z
  www.users.on.net/proformat/wicnames1.html
  i.e. Co. Wicklow

9. Births, Marriages and Deaths

Introductions

- Civil Records: Birth, Marriage and Death Registration
  www.from-ireland.net/gene/civilregistration.htm

- Civil Registration
  freepages.genealogy.rootsweb.com/~irishancestors/
                                    Civil%20registration.html

- Ginni Swanton's Web Site: Irish Birth, Death, and Marriage Civil Records
  www.ginnisw.com/irish3.htm

- The General Register Office
  www.groireland.ie

- A guide to the General Register Office of Ireland
  homepage.eircom.net/~seanjmurphy/gro/

- Ireland: Superintendent Registrars Districts by County
  www.rootsweb.com/~bifhsusa/irishregnc.html

- Records of Births, Marriages and Deaths
  www.nationalarchives.ie/birthsmarrdeaths.html
  From the National Archives

- State Registration of Births Marriages and Deaths
  scripts.ireland.com/ancestor/browse/records/state

- Irish Civil Records at the General Register Office
  www.genealogy.ie/categories/grorecs/

- Official Records of Births Marriages and Deaths
  www.genealogy.ie/categories/bmd/

- General Register Office (Northern Ireland)
  www.groni.gov.uk

- How to Order B/M/D
  www.rootsweb.com/~irllex/howto.htm

- Film Numbers for L.D.S. Index to their Irish B.D.M. Films
  www.rootsweb.com/~fianna/guide/lds-bdm.html
  List of microfilms of civil registration indexes 1864-1921

- Irish Birth Films 1864-1955
  www.genfindit.com/ibirths.htm
  Civil registration post 1864 at the Latter Day Saints

- Ireland Marriages L.D.S. Film Numbers
  www.genfindit.com/imarrs.htm
  Civil registration post 1845

- Ireland Death: L.D.S. Film Numbers
  www.genfindit.com/ideaths.htm
  Civil registration post 1864

- Civil Registration in Ireland: bringing Civil Registration into the 21st Century
  www.dun-laoghaire.com/genealogy/civreg.html
  Submission to an official inquiry

Parish Registers

- Churches and Searches
  www.rootsweb.com/~fianna/county/churches.html
  Searching in church registers

- Church of Ireland Parish Registers
  www.local.ie/content/25647.shtml/genealogy
  General introduction

- Parish Registers of the Churches
  freepages.genealogy.rootsweb.com/~irishancestors/
                                    Parish%20registers.html

- C.M.C.
  www.cmrcp.net
  Christenings, marriages and cemetery records; county pages listed below. Also includes some extracts from other records

- LDS Film Numbers for Ireland Parish Registers
  www.rootsweb.com/~fianna/county/ldspars.html

- Parish Registers in the National Library of Ireland
  www.nli.ie/pdfs/famil2.pdf
  General discussion

- Church of Ireland Index
  proni.nics.gov.uk/records/private/cofiindx.htm
  List of microfilmed parish registers (not indexed by personal name) at the Public Record Office of Northern Ireland

- Parish Register Copies in the Library of the Society of Genealogists: Ireland
  www.sog.org.uk/prc/irl.html
  List

- Ireland I.G.I. Batch Numbers
  freepages.genealogy.rootsweb.com/~hughwallis/IGIBatchNumbers/
  CountryIreland.htm

- Methodist Church Registers
  www.local.ie/content/25649.shtml
  General introduction

- Presbyterian Church Registers
  www.local.ie/content/25648.shtml/genealogy

- Roman Catholic Records
  scripts.ireland.com/ancestor/browse/counties/rcmaps/
  Comprehensive listing of registers for every Irish parish

National Databases

- The All Ireland Birth/Death Indices
  www.irelandgenweb.com/~cavan/all_ireland_indices.html
  Index to civil registration records for 1864

- Ireland Births or Baptisms, Deaths & Marriages Exchange
  www.thauvin.net/chance/ireland/bmd/

- Irish Church Records: Baptisms and Marriages
  freepages.genealogy.rootsweb.com/~irishchurchrecords/
  Database with entries contributed by users

- Irish Marriages 1771-1812
  www.ancestry.com/search/db.aspx?dbid=6404

- Marriages from the Master Marriage Index
  www.ajmorris.com/dig/toc/__000mmi.htm
  Index to marriages of persons with Irish surnames; source indexed not stated

- Irish Index
  www.irishindex.ca/
  15,000 birth, marriage and death announcements from *Freemans journal,* 1817-23

- Irish Marriages: being an index to the marriages in *Walker's Hibernian Magazine* 1771 to 1812
  home.att.net/~labaths/irish-marriages.htm

- Index to the births marriages and deaths in *Anthologia Hibernica,* 1793-1794
  home.att.net/~cmlabath/anthologia__hibernica.htm

County and Local Pages

Antrim
- County Antrim Roman Catholic Records
  www.rootsweb.com/~fianna/county/antrim/antrc.html

Island Magee
- Island Magee parish marriage records
  www.britishislesgenweb.org/northernireland/antrim/islandmagee.html
  19th c.

Carlow
- County Carlow Church of Ireland Records
  www.rootsweb.com/~fianna/county/carlow/carcoi.html
  List with locations

Fenagh
- Catholic Parish Registers of Fenagh and Myshall, Co. Carlow, Ireland, 1822-1880
  www.rootsweb.com/~irlcar2/fenagh.htm

Myshall *See* Fenagh

Cavan
- Listing of Church of Ireland Baptismal Registers for County Cavan
  freepages.genealogy.rootsweb.com/~adrian/Cav__CIB1.htm
- Church of Ireland Records
  www.sierratel.com/colinf/genuki/CAV/Cofl.htm
  Directory of microfilmed/indexed baptism, marriage and burial registers for Co. Cavan
  For Methodist registers, see **/Methodist.htm**
  For Presbyterian registers, see **/Presby.htm**
  For Quaker registers, see **/Quaker.html**
  For Roman Catholic registers, see **/RC.htm**
- Listing of Roman Catholic Baptismal Registers for County Cavan
  freepages.genealogy.rootsweb.com/~adrian/Cav__RCB1.htm

Ashfield
- Ashfield Parish, Co. Cavan Baptismal Register (1821-1864)
  freepages.genealogy.rootsweb.com/~adrian/Ash__Bap1.htm
  See also **/Ash__Bap2.htm**

- Ashfield Parish Area of Co. Cavan. Partial Marriage Register (1845-1917)
  freepages.genealogy.rootsweb.com/~adrian/Ash__Mar1.htm

Drumgoon
- Drumgoon Parish Area of Co. Cavan. Baptismal Register Extracts (1802-1864)
  freepages.genealogy.rootsweb.com/~adrian/Dgn__Bap2.htm
  Brief

Drung
- L.D.S. Parish Register Printouts. Drung Parish, Co. Cavan. Christenings 1735-1827
  freepages.genealogy.rootsweb.com/~adrian/LDSBap01.htm

Enniskeen *See also* Kilbride

- Deaths in Roman Catholic Parish of Enniskeen, Kingscourt, County Cavan, Ireland
  www.irelandgenweb.com/~cavan/enniskeen-deaths.html
  For Enniskeen 1846-50, and Kingscourt 1848-50

Kilbride
- Parish Register for the Diocese of Meath, Parishes of Kilbride & Mountnugent (Civil Parishes of Enniskeen, Kilbride and Loughan)
  www.rootsweb.com/~irleav/bride.htm
  For 1832-4

Kingscourt *See also* Enniskeen

- Extractions from Immaculate Conception Roman Catholic Church, Kingscourt, Bailieborough Poor Law Union, 1864-1877
  www.irelandgenweb.com/~cavan/imacconception.html

Loughan
  See Kilbride

Mountnugent
  See Kilbride

Clare

- Baptisms, Marriage and other Records: Co. Clare
  www.rootsweb.com/~irlcla/Surname.html

- County Clare Church of Ireland Parish Registers
  home.pacbell.net/nymets11/genuki/CLA/COIrecordsi.htm

- County Clare CMC Record Project
  www.cmcrp.net/Clare/

- County Clare Roman Catholic Parish Registers, with earliest recorded date
  home.pacbell.net/nymets11/genuki/CLA/RCrecords.htm

- Birth Announcements, co. Clare, 1827-1878
  www.otherdays.com/presentation/asp/search/
  presAffOther.asp?dbid=153
  Pay per view database; newspaper index

- Marriage Announcements, co. Clare, 1827-1845
  www.otherdays.com/presentation/asp/search/
  presAffOther.asp?dbid=155
  Pay per view database; newspaper index

- Death Announcements, co. Clare, 1827-1845
  www.otherdays.com/presentation/asp/search/
  presAffOther.asp?dbid=154
  Pay per view database; newspaper index

Killard

- Co. Clare Baptisms: Killard/Kilrush/Kilmurry/Kilmacduane
  freepages.genealogy.rootsweb.com/~msjenkins/records/clarebap.htm

Kilmaley

- Kilmaley Parish Baptism Records, County Clare, Ireland
  www.rootsweb.com/~irlcla/Kilmaley.html
  For 1882-90. Continued for 1891-8 at **/Kilmaley2.html**
  and for 1899-1900 at **/Kilmaley3.html**

Kilmihil

- Failte go dti Cill Michil: Genealogy
  www.kilmihil.com
  Click on 'Genealogy' for indexes to registers of Kilmihil

Liscannor

- Deaths in the Liscannor Area 1864-1870
  www.clarelibrary.ie/eolas/coclare/genealogy/
  deaths__in__the__liscannor__area.htm
  From civil registers

Cork

- County Cork Civil Registrations
  www.sci.net.au/userpages/mgrogan/Cork/a__civil.htm
  Many pages of indexes to and extracts from civil registration for particular places

- Cork: From Ireland
  www.from-ireland.net/contents/corkcontents.htm

- County Cork CMC Record Project
  www.cmcrp.net/Cork/
  Christenings, marriages and cemetery records

Ballymoney

- Ballymoney Parish Records 1805-1873
  www.paulturner.ca/Ireland/Cork/Ballymoney%20Parish/BP-text-1.htm

Ballyneen

- Ballyneen District Deaths by surname
  www.ginnisw.com/
  From the civil registers 1864-70

Bandon

- Births registered in Bandon. Co. Cork 1870
  uk.geocities.com/irishancestralpages/bandon1870b.html

Enniskeane

- Ginni Swanton's Web Site: Deaths from Enniskeane Parish Register and Ahiohill Cemetery
  www.ginnisw.com/Deaths%20Enniskeane%20Ahiohill.htm

Inchigeelagh

- Inchigeelagh Church Records, Co. Cork, from O'Kief, Coshe Mang, Slieve Lougher & Upper Blackwater in Ireland 1816 thru 1900
  www.sci.net.au/userpages/mgrogan/cork/inch__m.htm
  Marriages

Kinneigh

- Kinneigh Parish Records 1795-1854
  www.paulturner.ca/Ireland/Cork/Kinneigh__Parish/KP%20text%201.htm

Ovens

- Marriages: Parish of Ovens, Co. Cork
  www.sci.net.au/userpages/mgrogan/cork/ovens.htm
  For 1839-47

Donegal

- Church Records of County Donegal
  donegal.local.ie/content/28616.shtml/genealogy/
  overview__of__records
  List of registers of the Church of Ireland and the Roman Catholic church, with locations.

Cloncha

- Cloncha Parish births 1669 to 1783: extracts from the parish registers
  freepages.genealogy.rootsweb.com/~donegal/clonchareg.htm

Crossroads

- Crossroads Presbyterian Church, County Donegal, Ireland: Church Records
  mcn.ie/crossroads/genealogy/intro.htm
  Births from 1811, deaths 1854-95, marriages, 19-20th c.

Raphoe

- Union of Strabane Death Index ... Deaths Registered in the District of Raphoe
  freepages.genealogy.rootsweb.com/~donegaleire/Raphdeath.html
  For 1866-7

Down

Newry

- Partial Newry Marriage & Baptism Records from L.D.S. Microfilm
  freepages.genealogy.rootsweb.com/%7Edonaghmore1/newrymarbap.html
  For 1784-1820

Dublin

- County Dublin: Church of Ireland Records
  www.rootsweb.com/~fianna/county/dublin/dubcoi.html
  List with locations

- County Dublin C.M.C. Record Project
  cmcrp.net/Dublin
  i.e. christenings, marriages, and cemetery records. Contributed entries.

Fermanagh

- County Fermanagh Roman Catholic Parish Records
  www.genuki.org.uk/big/irl/FER/RCRecords.html

Devenish

- Devenish Baptisms
  www.fermanagh.org.uk/fermanaghpresents/devenish1.htm

Enniskillen

- Enniskillen 1600
  www.fermanagh.org.uk/fermanaghpresents/enniskillen.htm
  Baptisms, 17-18th c.

Inishmacsaint
- Inishmacsaint Baptisms
  www.fermanagh.org.uk/fermanaghpresents/inishmacl.htm
  For 1800-1814

Lisnaskea
- Index to Register of Baptisms, Marriages, Burials & Publications of Banns in the Parish of Lisnaskea in the County of Fermanagh and Diocese of Clogher
  www.ulsterancestry.com/BDM__Clogher.html
  Early 19th c.

Galway

Beagh
- Beagh Parish Catholic Baptisms 1855-1856
  home.att.net/~labaths/births.htm

Cummer
- Tuam Diocese: Cummer Parish
  pw2.netcom.com/~lgb1/tuamcumm.html
  Marriages 1813-16

- Marriages of Parish Cummer, Diocese Tuam
  www.rootsweb.com/~irlcnn/Tuam/Marriages/Marriages.htm
  For 1813-16 at present

Loughrea
- Loughrea Cathedral Baptisms 1852
  www.celticcousins.net/ireland/loughrea.htm

- Deaths registered in the District of Loughrea in the Union of Loughrea in the County of Galway
  www.rootsweb.com/~irlgal/index9.html

Moyrus
- Marriages - Parish Register, Catholic Chapelry of Roundstone, parish of Moyrus, Galway 1888-1889
  www.rootsweb.com/~irlgal/index10.html

Kerry
- Registration Districts in County Kerry
  homepage.eircom.net/~dinglemaps/genuki/KER/Regdists.html

- County Kerry CMC Record Projet
  www.cmcrp.net/Kerry/

- Family History Center Library Catalog Parish Register Film Numbers for County Kerry
  www.rootsweb.com/~irlker/parfilm.html

- On-Line Searchable Database
  www.rootsweb.com/~irlker/addrecords.html
  For Co. Kerry baptisms and marriages

- Baptisms/Birth Records
  www.rootsweb.com/~irlker/birth.html
  Contributed records for Co. Kerry

- Marriage Records, County Kerry, Ireland
  www.rootsweb.com/~irlker/marriage.html
  Contributed records

- Burial/Death Records
  www.rootsweb.com/~irlker/burial.html
  Contributed records for Co. Kerry

Ballyferriter
- Ballyferriter Church Records
  www.geocities.com/Athens/Ithaca/7974/Ballyferriter/church/
  Includes contributed records

Castle Island
- Baptism Locations in Castleisland Roman Catholic Parish
  www.rootsweb.com/~irlker/casparc.html

Keel

- Catholic Parish of Keel and Kiltallagh, Co. Kerry: Marriage Records 1804-1820
  www.shopshamrock.com/genealogy/keel/keel.php3

Kiltallagh

  See Keel

Lisselton

- Deaths, Lisselton Area
  www.geocities.com/dalyskennelly__2000/deathslisselton.html
  Late 20th c

Trughanacmy

- An Extract of Kerry Marriages in the Barony of Trughanacmy
  www.geocities.com/irishancestralpages/KMmain.html
  1874-84

- Kerry Marriages for the Barony of Trughanacmy 1877
  www.geocities.com/irishancestralpages/km1877p1.html
  Contined at /km1877p2.html
  See also familytreemaker.genealogy.com/users/o/r/o/
  Philip-J-Orourke/FILE/0026page.html

Kildare

- Church of Ireland Parish Registers
  Kildare.ie/library/KildareHeritage/page5.html
  For Co. Kildare

- Roman Catholic Parish Registers
  Kildare.ie/library/KildareHeritage/page4.html
  List for Co. Kildare

Ardkell

- Baptisms 1899-1916 for the Townland of Ardkell
  pw2.netcom.com/~lgb1/Ardkell.htm

Kilkenny

- County Kilkenny, Ireland, Civil Parish Records
  www.rootsweb.com/~irlkik/careclds.htm
  List

- County Kilkenny Catholic Parish Records: Catholic Parish to Civil Parish cross-reference with dates of earliest Catholic parish records
  www.rootsweb.com/~irlkik/carerecord.htm

Kilkenny

- St. John's (Maldin Street), Kilkenny
  www.rootsweb.com/~fianna/county/kilkenny/kik-mar3.html#bap
  Baptisms 1789-1841; Marriages 1790-1875

- St. Mary's, Kilkenny
  www.rootsweb.com/~fianna/county/kilkenny/kik-mar2.html#bap
  Baptisms 1772-1887; marriages 1755-1858.

- St. Patrick's, Kilkenny Marriages 1800's
  www.rootsweb.com/~fianna/county/kilkenny/kik-mar1.html

Kilmacow

- Kilmacow Parish Birth Index, County Kilkenny, Ireland (1858 to 1880)
  www.rootsweb.com/~irlkik/records/kilmindx.htm

Limerick

- Civil Parishes of County Limerick
  www.connorsgenealogy.com/LIM/Parishes.html
  List with notes on registers

- County Limerick CMC Record Project
  www.cmcrp.net/Limerick

Londonderry

- Derry: Roman Catholic Parish Records
  www.thauvin.net/chance/ireland/derry/rcparish.jsp
  At the Family History Library

Clonmany

- Roman Catholic Marriages for the Parish of Clonmany (1852-1900)
  www.iol.ie/~inishowen/genealogy/records/Clonmany/Marriage/

Longford

- Church Records
  www.rootsweb.com/~irllog/churchrecs.htm
  Indexes of various registers

- County Longford Roman Catholic Parish Records
  personal.nbnet.nb.ca/tmoffatt/RCfilmsLDS.html
  List of LDS films available

- Church Records
  www.rootsweb.com/~irllog/churchrecs.htm
  Includes Killoe marriages, 1826-1917, baptisms 1826-1917, and deaths 1826-84; Clonbroney marriages 1828-99, marriages 1828-99 and deaths, 1828-92; Granard marriages 1778-1894, baptisms 1811-65 and deaths 1811-65; Ardagh & Mowdow marriages 1792-1895, baptisms 1793-1895 and deaths 1822-95; Kilcommock marriages 1859-80, baptisms 1859-80, and deaths 1859-80.

Louth

Collon

- Collon-Dundalk Burials
  www.jbhallfreeservers.com/Collon%20-%20Louth%20Burials.htm/
  Collon parish burials 1791-1823; Dundalk, 1790-1802

Dundalk

See Collon

Mayo

- County Mayo CMC Record Project
  www.cmcrp.net/Mayo

- County Mayo Roman Catholic Church Records
  www.geocities.com/Heartland/Acres/4031/RCPARISH.HTML
  List of LDS films

- Births and Baptisms in Parishes Westport - Castlebar, Co. Mayo & area
  freepages.genealogy.rootsweb.com/~deesegenes/birth.html
  Extensive; covers many parishes, as does the following:

- Marriages in Parishes of Castlebar - Westport - Louisburg, Ballintober-Achill, Co. Mayo area
  freepages.genealogy.rootsweb.com/~deesegenes/marr.html

Claremorris

- Baptisms: Mayo Abbey, Claremorris, 1841
  pw2.netcom.com/~lgb1/MayoAbby.html

Glanduff

- Baptisms: Glanduff, Co. Mayo, 1872-1879
  www.geocities.com/Heartland/Acres/4031/Glanduff.html

Kilfian

- Kilfian Parish Killala Deaths
  freepages.genealogy.rootsweb.com/~deesegenes/kildeath.html

Kiltimagh

- Kiltimagh, Co. Mayo church records: baptisms July 1861 to September 1880
  www.rootsweb.com/~fianna/county/mayo/kiltimaghb.html

- Kiltimagh, Co. Mayo, Roman Catholic Marriages
  www.rootsweb.com/~fianna/county/mayo/maymar2.html

Roundfort

- Roundfort Parish, Co. Mayo
  pw2.netcom.com/~lgb1/Ardkell.html
  Baptisms 1899-1916

Westport

- Westport Parish Marriages 1823 to 1903
  freepages.genealogy.rootsweb.com/~deesegenes/wpt.htm

Monaghan

- Church Registers for County Monaghan
  www.exis.net/ahd/monaghan/churchregisters.htm

County Monaghan Roman Catholic Records available in the Mormons FHC
www.exis.net/ahd/monaghan/fhc-rc.htm

Roscommon

- Roscommon: Irish Parish Registers
www.rootsweb.com/~irlros/irish__parish__registers.htm
List

Roscommon

- Deaths from the Roscommon Town workhouse
www.geocities.com/Heartland/Pines/7030/page2.html
List for mid-late 19th c.

Sligo

- I.G.I. Extracts of Sligo County
www.rootsweb.com/~irlsli/index2.html

Castleconnor

- Castleconnor Parish Records
www.rootsweb.com/~irlsli/castelconnoropen.html

Kilglass

- Kilglass Parish, Co. Sligo
www.puregolduk.com/bren/kilglass__co__sligo3.htm
Index to baptisms

- Kilglass Marriages prior to 1850
www.puregolduk.com/bren/kilglass__co__sligo4.htm

- Some Death Records of Kilglass Parish from March 1825 to June 1867
www.puregolduk.com/bren/kilglass__co__sligo9.htm

Tipperary

- County Tipperary CMC Record Project
www.cmcrp.net/Tipperary
Christenings, marriage and cemetery records

- User Contributed Tipperary Baptisms
www.rootsweb.com/~irltip2/bap/

- Tipperary Family History Research
www.tfhr.org/
Holds the sacramental registers of the Roman Catholic Archdiocese of Cashel, and Diocese of Emly (46 parishes)

Carrick on Suir

- Births Registered in Carrick-On-Suir, Tipperary 1871
www.geocities.com/irishancestralpages/cosbi1871.html

- Baptisms, Carrick-on-Suir: extracts from the Roman Catholic Parochial Registers of Carrick-on-Suir, 1788-1851
www.rootsweb.com/~irltip2/carrick__bap.htm

- Some Marriages from Carrick-on-Suir 1788-1805
www.rootsweb.com/~irltip2/carrick__mar.htm

Clonmel

- Clonmel Births 1864-79
freepages.genealogy.rootsweb.com/~irish/clonmel/clonbirt.htm

Tyrone

- Church Records by Parish
freepages.genealogy.rootsweb.com/~cotyroneireland/
churchrecord/parishrecords.html

Arboe

- Arboe Roman Catholic Baptism Records
freepages.genealogy.rootsweb.com/~tyrone/church/churchrec/
arboe-rc-bapt.html

Coagh

- Coagh Civil Births
freepages.genealogy.rootsweb.com/~cotyroneireland/births/coagh.html
Late 19th c.

- Coagh Roman Catholic Baptism Records
  freepages.genealogy. Rootsweb.com/~cotyroneireland/births/
  coagh-rc.html

Donemana

- Donemana Records
  freepages.genealogy.rootsweb.com/~cotyroneireland/
  churchrecord/donemana.html

- Transcription of Donemana Presbyterian Registers
  freepages.genealogy.rootsweb.com/~cotyroneireland/churchrecord/
  donemanapresbreg.html

  For 1861-89

Kildress

- Kildress Roman Catholic Church Records
  freepages.genealogy.rootsweb.com/~cotyroneireland/churchrecord/
  kildressrc.htm

  Baptisms, 19th c.

Killyman

- Killyman Baptism Records
  freepages.genealogy.rootsweb.com/~cotyroneireland/churchrecord/
  killyman.html

  For 1841-71

- Killyman Burial Records
  freepages.genealogy.rootsweb.com/~cotyroneireland/churchrecord/
  killyman2.html

  For 1837-62

- [Killyman Baptisms, Church of Ireland, 1690-1898]
  freepages.genealogy.rootsweb.com/~cotyroneireland/churchrecord/
  killymanbaptisms.html

- [Killyman Marriages, Church of Ireland, 1757-1844]
  freepages.genealogy.rootsweb.com/~cotyroneireland/churchrecord/
  killymanmarriages.html

- [Killyman Burials, Church of Ireland, 1776-1877]
  freepages.genealogy.rootsweb.com/~cotyroneireland/churchrecord/
  killymanburials.html

Magheramason

- Magheramason Presbyterian Church Marriages, 1881-1927
  freepages.genealogy.rootsweb.com/~cotyroneireland/churchrecord/
  magheramason1881-1927.html

Waterford

- County Waterford CMC Record Project
  www.cmcrp.net/Waterford

Westmeath

Mullingar

- Church of Ireland Records: Mullingar 1877-1900
  www.rootsweb.com/~irlwem2/mullingar.htm

Wexford

- Extracts from the Marriages & Baptisms Registers of County Wexford
  home.att.net/~mayoireland/miscrecs3.htm
  From many parishes

- County Wexford CMC Record Project
  www.cmcrp.net/Wexford/

Wicklow

- County Wicklow CMC Record Project
  www.cmcrp.net/Wicklow
  Christenings, marriages and cemetery records

Arklow

- Peggy Leonards Christening Records of Arklow Parish, Wicklow
  www.cmcrp.net/Wicklow/ArklowB1.htm
  19-20th c. index

- County Wicklow: Arklow Parish Marriage Records
  www.cmcrp.net/Wicklow/ArklowM1.htm
  18-20th c. index

10. Monumental Inscriptions

Introductions

Cemetery Records
www.rootsweb.com/~fianna/guide/cemetery.html
Brief introduction

Cemetery Records Online
www.interment.net/ireland/
Directory, with numerous transcriptions of records, mostly listed below

Guide to Gravestone Inscriptions
proni.nics.gov.uk/records/graves.htm

Gravestone Records
scripts.ireland.com/ancestor/browse/records/graveyard
Introduction

International Association of Jewish Genealogical Societies: Cemetery Project: Ireland
www.jewishgen.org/cemetery/brit/ireland.html

Saving Graves Ireland
www.savinggraves-uk.org/ireland/
Preservation and restoration of graveyards

Understanding the Stones
proni.nics.gov.uk/records/stones.htm

Ireland
www.mbs-brasses.co.uk/bibliography__Foreign#Ireland
Bibliography of monumental brasses

Databases & Collections

History from Headstones
www.historyfromheadstones.com/
Database of 60,000+ Northern Ireland monumental inscriptions

- Irelands Gravestone Index
  www.irishgenealogy.ie/gravestones/
  Nearly 400,000 inscriptions from 851 cemeteries in ten Irish counties, and growing (mainly Northern Ireland)
- Churches & Cemeteries
  homepage.eircom.net/%7Ekevm/Churches.htm
  Pages for 23 places in various counties, mostly listed individually below
- Cemetery Headstone Transcriptions, Ireland
  members.iinet.net.au/~sgrieves/cemeteries__ireland.htm
  Transcriptions from cemeteries in Tipperary, Waterford, Tyrone, Londonderry, Leitrim, *etc.*
- Gravestone Transcriptions
  www.from-ireland.net/contents/graves.htm
  Numerous pages of transcriptions, mostly listed below
- Irish Cemetery Records
  www.scotlandsclans.com/ircemeteries.htm
  Links to numerous transcripts of inscriptions, etc.
- Irish Memorials of Dead
  www.ajmorris.com/dig/toc/memdead.htm
  Pay per view site. Index to tombstone inscriptions collected in the 19th c.

County and Local Pages
Antrim
Aughnhoy
- Aughnahoy
  www.from-ireland.net/graves/aughnahoyantrim.htm
  Inscriptions

Belfast
- The History of Clifton Street Graveyard
  www.glenravel.com/cliftonstreet.htm
  Includes inscriptions

Billy
- Gravestone Inscriptions at the Old Burying Ground Beside Billy Parish Church in North Antrim
  www.rootsweb.com/~irlantbp

Layde

- Layde Graveyard
  www.from-ireland.net/graves/taydeantrim.htm
  Inscriptions

Armagh

Armagh

- Gravestone Inscriptions, Sandy Hill Graveyard, Armagh City
  www.from-ireland.net/graves/sandyhillarmagh.htm

Creggan

- Inscriptions in Creggan Graveyard
  www.from-ireland.net/graves/cregganarmagh.htm

Crossmaglen

- Creggan Graveyard in Crossmaglen, Armagh County
  www.from-ireland.net/graves/creggancrossmaglenant.htm

Carlow

- Carlow Old Graves
  www.rootsweb.com/~irlcar2/Old__Graves.htm
  Index to transcripts of inscriptions

- Miscellaneous County Carlow Inscriptions
  www.from-ireland.net/graves/carlowmisc.htm

Dunleckney

- Carlow: Dunleckney Cemetery: Some Tombstone Inscriptions
  www.ajmorris.com/dig/fap/rec/
  Click on title. Registration needed

Hacketstown

- Hacketstown Cemetery, Hacketstown, County Carlow, Ireland
  www.interment.net/data/ireland/carlow/hacketstown/hacket.htm

Killerig

- Memorials of the Dead, Killerig & Tullow Churchyards
  www.rootsweb.com/~irlcar2/memorials.htm

Old Leighlin

- Saint Lazerian Churchyard, Old Leighlin, County Carlow, Ireland
  www.interment.net/data/ireland/carlow/lazerian/

Cavan

Ballyhaise

- Baillyhaise Cemetery
  www.sierratel.com/colinf/genuki/CAV/Castleterra/

  BallyhaiseCemetery.html

  List of family plots

Killeshandra

- Inscriptions in Killeshandra Old Cemetery
  homepages.iol.ie/~galwill/histtomb.htm

Knocktemple

- Knocktemple Old Cemetery Inscriptions, County Cavan, Ireland
  www.ancestry.com/search/rectype/inddbs/4225.htm

Maghera

- Maghera Cemetery, County Cavan, Ireland
  www.interment.net/data/ireland/cavan/maghera/maghera.htm

Mullagh

- Teampall Cheallaigh Cemetery, Mullagh, County Cavan, Ireland
  www.interment.net/data/ireland/cavan/teampall__heallaigh/teampall.htm

Templeport

- Inscriptions in Templeport Cemetery
  www.stpeter.utvinternet.com/headstones.htm
  See also **/memorialindex.htm**

Virginia

- Church of Ireland Churchyard, Virginia, County Cavan, Ireland
  www.interment.net/data/ireland/cavan/coi__virginia/

- The Old Cemetery, Virginia, County Cavan, Ireland
  www.interment.net/data/ireland/cavan/old/

- Raffony Graveyard, Virginia, County Cavan, Ireland
  www.interment.net/data/ireland/cavan/raffony/raffony.htm

Clare

- Graveyard Inscriptions
  www.rootsweb.com/~irlcla/graveyardinscriptions.html
  Surname index to transcriptions at the East Clare Heritage Centre

- Memorials of the Dead, West Clare
  www.from-ireland.net/graves/clarewestgraves.htm
  Surname index to published transcriptions

- Monumental Inscriptions from Co. Clare Graveyards
  home.att.net/~wexlababe/table__ofcontents.htm/
  #Graveyard%20Inscriptions
  For Teample Bridgetown, O'Briensbridge and Punchbowl. Click on title

Cork

- Cork Graveyards and Published Transcriptions
  freepages.genealogy.rootsweb.com/~colin/Ireland/CorkGraveyards.htm

Adrigole

- Adrigole Memorial Inscriptions, R.C.
  www.from-ireland.net/graves/adrigoletrans.htm
  Inscriptions

Aghinagh

- Cork Gravestones Name Index: Aghinagh
  www.from-ireland.net/graves/aghinaghindex.htm

Carrigrohanebeg

- Cork Gravestones Index to Names: Carrigrohanebeg
  www.from-ireland.net/graves/carrigrohanebegindex.htm

Churchtown
See Doneraile

Clonmult

- Cork Gravestones Name Index: Clonmult
  www.from-ireland.net/graves/clonmultindex.htm

Dangandonovan

- Cork Gravestones Name Index: Dangandonovan
  www.from-ireland.net/graves/dangandonindex.htm

- Dangandonovan Cemetery
  www.sci.net.au/userpages/mgrogan/cork/dangandonovan.htm

Doneraile

- Cemetery Inscriptions from Casey vol.11. Old Court Cemetery, Doneraile, Granard Cemetery, Liscarroll, Killabraher, Parish of Dromina, Exterior of Churchtown Church; Kilbrogan Cemetery, Co. Cork
  www.sci.net.au/userpages/mgrogan/cork/donraile.htm

Dromina
See Doneraile

Kilbehenny

- Kilbehenny Grave Inscriptions, Co. Cork
  www.sci.net.au/userpages/mgrogan/cork/kilbehenny.htm

Kilbrogan
See Doneraile

Killabraher
See Doneraile

Killeagh

- Cork Gravestones Name Index: Killeagh
  www.from-ireland.net/graves/killeaghindex.htm

- Killeagh Cemetery
  www.sci.net.au/userpages/mgrogan/cork/killeagh__cem.htm

- Gravestone Inscriptions, Killeagh Burial Ground, Co.Cork
  www.sci.net.au/userpages/mgrogan/cork/killeagh__grave.htm

Kilnaglory

- The Gravestone Inscriptions of Co. Cork, V: Kilnaglory Burial Ground
  www.from-ireland.net/graves/kilnaglorycork.htm
  Index to published transcription

Liscarrol

  See Doneraile

Mallow

- Grave Monuments, St. James Protestant Cemetery, Mallow, Co. Cork
  www.sci.net.au/userpages/mgrogan/cork/mallow__stj.htm

- Monument Inscriptions from St. Mary's Catholic Cemetery, Mallow, Co. Cork
  www.sci.net.au/userpages/mgrogan/cork/mallow__stm__grave.htm

Mologga

- Mologga Cemetery Inscriptions, Co. Cork
  www.sci.net.au/userpages/mgrogan/cork/mologga.htm

Rosscarbery

- Partial Transcription from the Old Cemetery in Rosscarbery Town
  members.cox.net/hayes1966/rosscem.htm

Tisaxon

- The Gravestone Inscriptions of Co. Cork, VII. Tisaxon Burial Ground
  www.from-ireland.net/graves/tisaxoncork.htm
  Index to published transcription

Donegal

- Cemeteries of Donegal
  freepages.genealogy.rootsweb.com/~donegaleire/Cemeteries.html

- Monumental Inscriptions
  freepages.genealogy.routsweb.com/~donegal/mis.htm
  General discussion with links to Donegal sites

Ballyshannon

- The Gravestone Inscriptions, St. Anne's Church of Ireland, Ballyshannon
  freepages.genealogy.rootsweb.com/~donegal/stanne.htm

- St. Anne's Church of Ireland, Ballyshannon, County Donegal, Ireland
  www.interment.net/data/ireland/donegal/st__anne.htm

- The Gravestone Inscriptions St. Annes Church of Ireland, Ballyshannon
  www.ulsterancestry.com/ua-free__GravestoneInscriptions.html

- Assaroe Abbey Cemetery, Ballyshannon
  freepages.genealogy.rootsweb.com/~donegal/assaroecem.htm

- Assaroe Abbey Cemetery, Ballyshannon
  www.ulsterancestry.com/
  Abbey__Cemetery__Inscriptions-Assaroe%20.html

Bundoran

- Finner, Bundoran
  freepages.genealogy.rootsweb.com/~donegal/finner.htm
  Monumental inscriptions

- Finner Graveyard, Bundoran, County Donegal
  www.interment.net/data/donegal/finner__graveyard.htm

Creeslough

- County Donegal, Ireland, Catholic Cemetery: Creeslough, County Donegal, Ireland
  www.geocities.com/Heartland/Estates/6587/Doncem.html

- Catholic Cemetery: Creeslough, County Donegal, Ireland
  www.geocities.com/Heartland/Estates/6587/Doncem.html

Gartan

- Gartan Graveyard, County Donegal, Ireland
  www.interment.net/data/ireland/donegal/gartan__graveyard.htm

- The Gravestone Inscriptions, Gartan Graveyard
  freepages.genealogy.rootsweb.com/~donegal/gartan/artgrave.htm

Inver

- Inver C.O.I. Cemetery
  freepages.genealogy.rootsweb.com/%7Edonegaleire/Inver.html

Killeshandra

- Inscriptions in Killeshandra Old Cemetery
  homepages.iol.ie/histtomb.htm

Letterkenny

- Leck Cemetery, Letterkenny, Donegal, Ireland
  freepages.genealogy.rootsweb.com/~donegaleire/Donleck.htm
  Gravestone Inscriptions

Tullaghobegley

- Tullaghobegley Graveyard
  freepages.genealogy.rootsweb.com/%7Edonegal/tullagrave.htm

- Magheragallon Old Graveyard, Tullaghobegley
  freepages.genealogy.rootsweb.com/~donegal/magheracem.htm

Down

- County Down Burial Index 1700s
  www.rootsweb.com/~nirdow2/Burial/down__index.htm
  Inscriptions

- County Down Graveyard Transcriptions Volume 2
  www.from-ireland.net/graves/downvol2.htm
  From 9 graveyards

Aghlisnafin

- Selected Tombstone Inscriptions from Aghlisnafin, County Down
  www.ajmorris.com/dig/fap/rec/
  Click on title

Dublin

- Monumental Brass Rubbings for Ireland: Dublin
  www.ashmole.co.uk/ash/departments/antiquities/brass/counties/
  Dublin.html

  In the Ashmolean Museum, Oxford

Ballbriggan

- Saints Peter and Paul Cemetery, County Dublin, Ireland
  www.interment.net/data/ireland/dublin/saintspp/saintspp.htm
  At Ballbriggan

Castleknock

- St. Bridget's Church of Ireland Cemetery, Castleknock, County Dublin,
  Ireland
  www.interment.net/data/ireland/dublin/stbridget/bridget.htm

Deans Grange

- Deans Grange Cemetery, County Dublin, Ireland
  www.interment.net/data/ireland/dublin/deans/dean__grange.htm

Donabate

- Saint Patrick Cemetery, Donabate, County Dublin, Ireland
  www.interment.net/data/ireland/dublin/stpat/stpat.htm

Dublin

- Names on Coffin Plates in the Vaults of St. Andrews Church, Westland
  Row, Dublin (R.C.)
  www.from-ireland.net/graves/standrewswestlandrowdublin.htm

Glasnevin

- Glasnevin Cemetery
  www.glasnevin-cemetery.ie/
  Includes detials of a project to create a database for 250,000 burial
  records

- Glasnevin Cemetery
  en.wikipedia.org/wiki/Glasnevin__Cemetery
  Encyclopedia article

- Glasnevin Cemetery, County Dublin, Ireland
  www.interment.net/data/ireland/dublin/glasnevin/glasnevin.htm

- Glasnevin Cemetery, Dublin
  www.from-ireland.net/graves/glasnevin.htm
  Transcription of 190+ inscriptions

Grallagh

- Grallagh Cemetery, Grallagh, County Dublin, Ireland
  www.interment.net/data/ireland/dublin/grallagh/grallagh.htm

Grangegorman

- Grangegorman Military Cemetery, County Dublin, Ireland
  www.interment.net/data/ireland/dublin/grangegorman/

Howth

- St. Mary's Cemetery, Howth, Co. Dublin, Ireland
  freepages.genealogy.rootsweb.com/~chrisu/howth2.htm

Lusk

- Lusk Old Churchyard Cemetery, County Dublin, Ireland
  www.interment.net/data/ireland/dublin/oldlusk/

Mulhuddart

- Mulhuddart Cemetery, County Dublin, Ireland
  www.interment.net/data/ireland/dublin/mulhuddart/mulhuddart.htm

Rush

- Kenure Cemetery, Rush, County Dublin, Ireland
  www.interment.net/data/ireland/dublin/kenure/kenure.htm

- Whitestown Cemetery, Rush, County Dublin, Ireland
  www.interment.net/data/dublin/whitestown/whitestown.htm

Saint Macullin

- Saint Macullin's Churchyard Cemetery, County Dublin, Ireland
  www.interment.net/data/ireland/dublin/macullin/macullin.htm

Skerries

- St. Patricks Holmpatrick Cemetery, Skerries, County Dublin, Ireland
  www.interment.net/data/ireland/dublin/patrick/holmpatrick.htm

Fermanagh

Aghalurcher

- Fermanagh Gravestones Name Index: Aghalurcher
  www.from-ireland.net/graves/aghalurcherferm.htm

Aghavea

- Fermanagh Gravestones Name Index: Aghavea
  www.from-ireland.net/graves/aghaveafermanagh.htm

Bannagh

- Bannagh Inscriptions
  www.fermanagh.org.uk/fermanaghpresents/banninscr.htm

Caldragh

- Caldragh Cemetery Inscriptions
  www.fermanagh.org.uk/fermanaghpresents/caldraghg1.htm

Collaghty

- Collaghty Church
  www.fermanagh.org.uk/fermanaghpresents/colaghty.htm

Donagh

- Fermanagh Gravestones: Name Index: Donagh
  www.from-ireland.net/graves/donaghferm.htm

Rosslea

- Fermanagh Gravestones Name Index. St. Tierney's, Rosslea
  www.from-ireland.net/graves/sttierneysferm.htm

Tirwinney
- Tirwinney Graveyard Inscriptions
  www.fermanagh.org.uk/fermanaghpresents/tirwinney.htm

Tubrid
- Tubrid Church of Ireland
  www.fermanagh.org.uk/fermanaghpresents/tubrid.htm
  Inscriptions

Tullynageeran
- Tullynageeran Inscriptions
  www.fermanagh.org.uk/fermanaghpresents/tully.htm

Galway

Beagh
- Inscriptions from Shanaglish, Beagh Parish, Galway
  home.att.net/~labaths/cembeagh.htm

Mullaghgloss
- Toorena Cemetery, Mullaghgloss, County Galway, Ireland
  www.interment.net/data/ireland/galway/toorena/toorena.htm

Oughterard
- Kilcummin Cemetery, Oughterard, County Galway, Ireland
  www.interment.net/data/ireland/galway/kilcummin/

Renvyle
- Renvyle Cemetery, Renvyle, County Galway, Ireland
  www.interment.net/data/ireland/galway/renvyle/renvyle.htm

Saint Brendan
- Christchurch Churchyard, Saint Brendan, County Galway, Ireland
  www.interment.net/data/ireland/galway/christchurch/

Kerry

Abbeydorney
- Gravestone Inscriptions, Abbeydorney, Co. Kerry
  kerry.local.ie/content/31975.html

Ardfert
- Gravestone Inscriptions, Ardfert, Co. Kerry
  kerry.local.ie/content/30238.shtml

Ballymacelligott
- O'Brennan Graveyard, Ballymacelligott, Kerry
  www.otherdays.com/presentation/asp/search/
  presAffOther.asp?dbid=174

  Pay per view database

Brosna
- Brosna Cemetery Inscriptions
  www.geocities.com/bluegumtrees/cemetery.html

Castleisland
- Dysert Graveyard, Castleisland, Co.Kerry
  www.otherdays.com/presentation/asp/search/
  presAffOther.asp?dbid=133

  Pay per view database

- Nohoval Graveyard, Castleisland, Co.Kerry
  www.otherdays.com/presentation/asp/search/
  presAffOther.asp?dbid=184

  Pay per view database

- Old Kibannivane Graveyard, Castleisland, Kerry
  www.otherdays.com/presentation/asp/search/
  presAffOther.asp?dbid=172

  Pay per view database

Currow
- Old Killeentierna Graveyard, Currow, Kerry
  www.otherdays.com/presentation/asp/search/
  presAffOther.asp?dbid=173

  Pay per view database

Killorglin

- Killorglin Tombstone Inscriptions
  www.rootsweb.com/~irlker/tombkillor.html

Knockbrack

- Burial Ground, Knockbrack
  www.from-ireland/net/graves/knockbrackinscrs.htm

Listowel

- Cemetery Inscriptions: Listowel Area
  www.rootsweb.com/~irlker/tomblist.html

Kildare

Ballymore Eustace

- Saint Mary Cemetery, Ballymore Eustace, County Kildare, Ireland
  www.interment.net/data/ireland/kildare/stmary/mary.htm

Bodenstown

- Bodenstown Churchyard Cemetery, Bodenstown, County Kildare, Ireland
  www.interment.net/data/ireland/kildare/bodenstown/bodenstown.htm

Celbridge

- Ladychapel Cemetery, Celbridge, County Kildare, Ireland
  www.interment.net/data/ireland/kildare/ladychapel/lady.htm

Clane

- Clane Abbey Cemetery, Clane Village, County Kildare, Ireland
  www.interment.net/data/ireland/kildare/clane__abbey/clane.htm

Eadestown

- Eadestown Cemetery, Eadestown, County Kildare, Ireland
  www.interment.net/data/ireland/kildare/easdestown/eadestown.htm

Enfield

- Kilshanroe Cemetery, Enfield, County Kildare
  www.interment.net/data/ireland/kildare/kilshanroe/kilshanroe.htm

Killybegs

- Kildare Gravestones Name Index: Killybegs, Old: Prosperous, Co. Kildare
  www.from-ireland.net/graves/kild/killybegs.htm

Naas

- Kildare Gravestones Name Index: St. David's, Naas, Co. Kildare
  www.from-ireland.net/graves/kild/stdavidsnaas.htm

Kilkenny

Bennettsbridge

- Bennettsbridge Cemetery, Bennettsbridge, County Kilkenny, Ireland
  www.interment.net/data/ireland/kilkenny/ben__bridge/

Clara

- Clara Churchyard Cemetery, Clara, County Kilkenny, Ireland
  www.interment.net/data/ireland/kilkenny/clara/clara.htm

Freshford

- Clontubrid Cemetery, Freshford, County Kilkenny, Ireland
  www.interment.net/data/ireland/kilkenny/clontubrid/

Kilkenny

- Saint John Churchyard, Kilkenny City, County Kilkenny, Ireland
  www.interment.net/data/ireland/kilkenny/stjohn/

Paulstown

- Paulstown New Cemetery, County Kilkenny, Ireland
  www.interment.net/data/ireland/kilkenny/paulstown/paulstown.htm

Saint Kieran

- Saint Kieran's Cemetery, County Kilkenny, Ireland
  www.interment.net/data/ireland/kilkenny/st__kierans/kieran.htm

Thomastown

- Saint Mary New Cemetery, Thomastown, County Kilkenny, Ireland
  www.interment.net/data/ireland/kilkenny/stmary/stmary.htm

- Thomastown Old Graveyard, County Kilkenny, Ireland
  www.interment.net/data/ireland/kilkenny/thomas__old/

Tullaherin
- Tullaherin Cemetery, Tullaherin, County Kilkenny, Ireland
  www.interment.net/data/ireland/kilkenny/tullaherin/tullaherin.htm

Laois

Abbey Leix
- County Laois Graveyards: Abbey Leix, Church of Ireland: Name Index
  www.from-ireland.net/graves/laois/abbeyleixcoi.htm

Aghaboe
- County Laois Graveyards, Ireland: Aghaboe
  www.from-ireland.net/graves/laois/aghaboe.htm

Aharney
- County Laois Graveyards, Ireland: Aharney: Name Index
  www.from-ireland.net/graves/laois/aharney.htm

Attanagh
- County Laois (Leix, Queen's) Ireland: Graveyards: Attanagh: Name Index
  www.from-ireland.net/graves/laois/attanagh.htm

Aughmacart
- County Laois Graveyards: Aughmacart: Name Index
  www.from-ireland.net/graves/laois/aughmacart.htm

Ballyadding
- County Laois Graveyards: Ballyadding: Name Index
  www.from-ireland.net/graves/laois/ballyadding.htm

Ballylynam
- County Laois Graveyards: Ballylynam: Name Index
  www.from-ireland.net/graves/laois/ballylynam.htm

Ballyroan
- County Laois Graveyards: Ballyroan: Name Index
  www.from-ireland.net/graves/laois/ballyroan.htm

Bawnhill
- County Laois Graveyards: Bawnhill: Name and Year Index - partial
  www.from-ireland.net/graves/laois/bawnhill.htm

Bordwell
- County Laois Graveyards: Bordwell: Name Index
  www.from-ireland.net/graves/laois/bordwell.htm

Camross
- County Laois Graveyards: Camross: Name Index
  www.from-ireland.net/graves/laois/camross.htm

Clough
- County Laois Graveyards: Clough: Name Index
  www.from-ireland.net/graves/laois/clough.htm

Coolkerry
- County Laois Graveyards: Coolkerry: Name Index
  www.from-ireland.net/graves/laois/coolkerry.htm

Dysart
- Memorials of the Dead: Dysart (Enos) Churchyard
  www.rootsweb.com/~irllex/memorials.htm

Errill
- County Laois Graveyards: Errill: Name Index
  www.from-ireland.net/graves/laois/errill.htm

Killinard
- Memorials of the Dead: Killinard Churchyard
  www.rootsweb.com/~irllex/memorials2.htm

Mountmellick

- Ivy Chapel Graveyard, Mountmellick, Co. Laois
  www.otherdays.com/presentation/asp/search/
  presAffOther.asp?dbid=134
  Pay per view database

Rahanavannagh

- County Laois Graveyards: Rahanavannagh: Name Index
  www.from-ireland.net/graves/laois/rahanavan.htm

Raheen

- County Laois Graveyards: Raheen: Name Index
  www.from-ireland.net/graves/laois/raheen.htm

Rathsaran

- Rathsaran/Rathsarne Memorial Inscriptions, Church of Ireland
  www.from-ireland.net/graves/rathsarantrans.htm

Leitrim

Kinlough

- Kinlough Graveyard, Kinlough, County Leitrim, Ireland
  www.interment.net/data/ireland/leitrim/kinlough.htm

Limerick

Ardagh

- Abbreviated Head Stone Inscriptions in Ardagh Cemetery
  home.att.net/%7Ewexlababe/abbreviated__headstone__inscriptions.htm

Ballyorgan

See Glenroe

Donaghmore

- Donaghmore Graveyard, Co. Limerick
  home.att.net/%7Ewexlababe/co__limerick__graveyards.htm

Glenroe

- Glenroe - Ballyorgan (Co.Limerick) Necrology List
  home.att.net/~wexlababe/graveyard__inscriptions.htm

Kilbeheny

- Monumental Inscriptions from the Civil Parish of Kilbeheny
  home.att.net/~wexlababe/monumental__inscriptions__kilbeheny.htm

Mount St. Lawrence

- Mount St. Lawrence Cemetery Records, Limerick, Ireland
  home.att.net/%7Ewexlababe/mt__st__lawrence__cemetery.htm

Rathkeale

- Rathkeale Graveyard, Co, Limerick
  home.att.net/~labaths/cemlim.htm

Londonderry

- County Derry Cemetery Project
  www.rootsweb.com/~nirldy2/cemindex.htm
  19 cemeteries; 'under construction'

Glendermot

See Tipperary. Dovea

Saint Patrick

- Saint Patrick Cemetery, County Derry, Northern Ireland
  www.interment.net/data/nire/derry/stpat/patrick.htm

- Saint Patrick Cemetery located near Sixtowns and Draperstown
  www.rootsweb.com/~nirldy2/St.__Patrick__Cem.htm

Longford

Drumlish

- Drumlish Old Cemetery, County Longford, Ireland
  www.interment.net/data/ireland/longford/drumlish/old.htm

Newtownbond

- Newtownbond Church Graveyard
  www.geocities.com/grymorgan

Lough

Ardee

- Monumental Inscriptions at old Saint Mary's, Ardee, Co. Louth
  www.from-ireland.net/graves/stmarysardeelouth.htm

Ballymakenny

- Gravestone Inscriptions in Ballymakenny, Co. Lough
  www.from-ireland.net/graves/ballymakennylouth.htm

Collon

- Collon Old Cemetery, County Louth, Ireland
  www.interment.net/data/ireland/Louth/collon/oldcollon.htm

Termonfeckin

- Monumental Inscriptions, Termonfeckin Cemetery, Co. Lough
  www.from-ireland.net/graves/termonlouth.htm

Mayo

- Extracts from Inscriptions in Westport - Castlebar area
  freepages.genealogy.rootsweb.com/~deesegenes/cem.html

Achill Island

- Sleivemore Old Cemetery, Achill Island, County Mayo, Ireland
  www.interment.net/data/ireland/mayo/sleivemore/sleivemore.htm

Aghagower

- Aghagower Cemetery
  freepages.genealogy.rootsweb.com/~deesegenes/ag.htm

Ballaghaderreen

- Kilcolman Old Cemetery, Ballaghaderreen, County Mayo, Ireland
  www.interment.net/data/ireland/mayo/kilcolman/oldkilman.htm

Ballindine

- New Cemetery, Ballindine, County Mayo, Ireland
  www.interment.net/data/ireland/mayo/newcem/new.htm

- Saint Joseph Churchyard Cemetery, Ballindine, County Mayo, Ireland
  www.interment.net/data/ireland/mayo/stjoe/

Ballinvilla

- Ballinvilla Graveyard, County Mayo, Ireland
  www.interment.net/data/ireland/mayo/ballinvilla/ballinvilla.htm

Bekan

- Bekan Cemetery, Bekan Village, County Mayo, Ireland
  www.interment.net/data/ireland/mayo/bekan/bekan.htm

Bohola

- Bohola Cemetery, County Mayo, Ireland
  www.interment.net/data/ireland/mayo/bohola/

Burrishoole

- Burrishoole Cemetery
  www.geocities.com/Heartland/Park/7461/graves.html/

Charlestown

- Charlestown
  homepage.eircom.net/%7Ekevm/Charlestown/Name__index.htm

- Bushfield Church, Charlestown, Co. Mayo
  homepage.eircom.net/%7Ekevm/Bushfield/bushfield__church.htm

Claremorris

- Saint Mary's Abbey Cemetery, Ballinasmala, Claremorris, County Mayo, Ireland
  www.interment.net/data/ireland/mayo/stmary/

- Saint Colman's Cemetery, Claremorris, County Mayo, Ireland
  www.interment.net/data/ireland/mayo/coleman/stcolman.htm

- Tulrahan Cemetery, Claremorris, County Mayo, Ireland
  www.interment.net/data/ireland/mayo/tulrahan.htm

Kilmovee

- Kilmovee
  homepage.eircom.net/%7Ekevm/Kilmovee/Kilmovee.htm
  Inscriptions

- Kilmovee Stained Glass Windows
  homepage.eircom.net/%7Ekevm/Kilmovee/Kilmovee.htm
  Inscriptions

Kiltimagh

- Kilkinure Cemetery, Kiltimagh, County Mayo, Ireland
  www.interment.net/data/ireland/mayo/kilkinure/kilkinure.htm

Meelick

- Meelick New Cemetery
  homepage.eircom.net/%7Ekevm/Meelick/New.htm
  List of inscriptions

- Meelick Old Cemetery
  homepage.eircom.net/%7Ekevm/Meelick/Old.htm
  List of inscriptions

Murrisk

- Gravestone Inscriptions, Murrisk, Co. Mayo
  www.sci.net.au/userpages/mgrogan/cork/murrisk.htm

Swinford

- Midfield Cemetery, Swinford, County Mayo, Ireland
  www.interment.net/data/ireland/mayo/midfield/

Meath

Ashbourne

- Church of the Immaculate Conception Churchyard, Ashbourne, County Meath, Ireland
  www.interment.net/data/ireland/meath/immaculate/conception.htm

- Greenogue Cemetery, Donaghmore, Ashbourne, County Meath, Ireland
  www.interment.net/data/ireland/meath/greenogue/greenogue.htm

Athboy

- County Meath Graveyards: Athboy: Name Index
  www.from-ireland.net/graves/meath/athboy.htm

Batterstown

- Batterstown Churchyard Cemetery, Batterstown, County Meath, Ireland
  www.interment.net/data/ireland/meath/batterstown/balterstown.htm

Clonalvy

- Clonalvy Cemetery, Clonalvy, County Meath, Ireland
  www.interment.net/data/ireland/meath/clonalvy/clonalvy.htm

Duleek

- Some Monumental Inscriptions from Duleek Church of Ireland, Co. Meath
  www
  www.from-ireland.net/graves/duleekchurchlanemeath.htm

Dunboyne

- County Meath Graveyards: Dunboyne, Church of Ireland Gravestones: Name Index
  www.from-ireland.net/graves/meath/dunboyne.htm

Dunshaughlin

- Dunshaughlin Cemetery, Dunshaughlin, County Meath, Ireland
  www.interment.net/data/ireland/meath/dunshaughlin/dunshaughlin.htm

Kells

- Some Monumental Inscriptions from Kells, Co. Meath
  www.from-ireland.net/graves/kellsmeath.htm

Kentstown

- Kentstown Churchyard Cemetery, Kentstown, County Meath
  www.interment.net/data/ireland/meath/kentstown/kents.htm

Kilmessen

- Kilmessen
  homepage.eircom.net/%7Ekevm/Kilmessan/
  List of inscriptions

Moy

- County Meath Graveyards: Moy, near Summerhill: Name Index
  www.from-ireland.net/graves/meath/moy.htm

Moyagher

- County Meath Graves: Moyagher: Name Index
  www.from-ireland.net/graves/meath/moyagher.htm

Moynalty
- Moynalty Cemetery, Moynalty, County Meath, Ireland
  www.interment.net/data/ireland/meath/moynalty/moynalty.htm

Oldcastle
- Loughcrew Saint Keverne Church of Ireland Cemetery, Oldcastle,
  County Meath
  www.interment.net/data/ireland/meath/loughcrew/loughcrew.htm

- Loughcrew Saint Oliver Plunkett Churchyard, Oldcastle, County Meath,
  Ireland
  www.interment.net/data/ireland/meath/plunkett/stoliver.htm

- Saint Bridget's Cemetery, Oldcastle, County Meath, Ireland
  www.interment.net/data/ireland/meath/stbridget/bridget.htm

Rathcore
- Rathcore Church of Ireland, Co. Meath: Church and Graveyard
  Inscriptions
  homepage.eircom.net/~Rathmolyongraveyard/directory/HOMER.html

Rathmolyon
- Rathmolyon Graveyard Inscriptions
  homepage.eircom.net/~Rathmolyongraveyard/directory/IndexRC.html

Monaghan

Clones
- Clones Round Tower Graveyard, Clones, Co. Monaghan
  www.from-ireland.net/graves/clonesroundtower.htm
  Monumental Inscriptions

Offaly

Lusmagh
- Kilmachonna, Lusmagh: Offaly Tombstone Inscriptions
  www.from-ireland.net/graves/kilmachonnaoffaly.htm

Roscommon

Athlone
- Drum Cemetery, Athlone, County Roscommon, Ireland
  www.rootsweb.com/~irish/igsi__published/cemetery/roscdrum.htm
  General discussion; no inscriptions

Baslic
- Baslic Cemetery
  homepage.eircom.net/~kevm/Baslic/Baslic__2.htm

Boyle
- Assylinn Cemetery, Boyle, County Roscommon, Ireland
  www.interment.net/data/ireland/roscommon/assylinn/assylinn.htm

- Estersnow Cemetery, Croghan, Boyle, County Roscommon, Ireland
  www.interment.net/data/ireland/roscommon/estersnow/estersnow.htm

- Kilnamanagh Cemetery, Boyle, County Roscommon, Ireland
  www.interment.net/data/ireland/roscommon/kilnamanagh/
                                           kilnamanagh.htm

Elphin
- Saint Patrick Churchyard Cemetery, Elphin Town, County Roscommon,
  Ireland
  www.interment.net/data/ireland/roscommon/stpat/stpat.htm

- Kiltrustan Cemetery, Elphin, County Roscommon, Ireland
  www.interment.net/data/ireland/roscommon/kiltrustan/kiltrustan.htm

Kilglass
- Kilglass Cemetery, Kilglass, County Roscommon, Ireland
  www.interment.net/data/ireland/roscommon/kilglass/kilglass.htm

Shankill
- Old Shankill Cemetery, Shankill, County Roscommon, Ireland
  www.interment.net/data/ireland/roscommon/oldshankhill.htm

Stokestown

- Stokestown Cemetery, Stokestown, County Roscommon, Ireland
  www.interment.net/data/ireland/roscommon/stokestown/stoke.htm

Tulsk

- Tulsk Cemetery, Tulsk Village, County Roscommon, Ireland
  www.interment.net/data/ireland/roscommon/tulsk/tulsk.htm

- Kilcooley Cemetery, Kilcooley, Tulsk, County Roscommon, Ireland
  www.interment.net/data/ireland/roscommon/kilcooley/kilcooley.htm

Sligo

- Burial in Sligo County, Ireland
  www.rootsweb.com/~irlsli/index2.html
  Monumental inscriptions for many cemeteries

Ahamlish

- Ahamlish
  homepage.eircom.net/Ahamlish/Ahamlish.htm

Ballisodare

- Old Ballisodare Cemetery, County Sligo, Ireland
  www.interment.net/data/ireland/sligo/ballisodare/ballisodare.htm

Ballygawley

- Ballygawley
  homepage.eircom.net/%7Ekevm/Ballygawley/Ballygawley.htm
  List of inscriptions at Kilross Cemetery

Banada Abbey

- Banada Abbey
  homepage.eircom.net/~kevm/Banada__Abby.htm
  Monumental inscriptions

Carrowanty

- Carrowanty Cemetery, County Sligo, Ireland
  www.interment.net/data/ireland/sligo/carrowanty/carrowanty.htm

Collooney

- Collooney Cemetery, Collooney, County Sligo, Ireland
  www.interment.net/data/ireland/sligo/collooney/collooney.htm

Curry

- Curry
  homepage.eircom.net/~kevm/Curry/Curry__Church.htm

Gurteen

- Gurteen Cemetery, Gurteen, County Sligo, Ireland
  www.interment.net/data/ireland/sligo/gurteen/gurteen.htm

Keelogues

- Keelogues
  homepage.eircom.net/%7Ekevm/Keelogues/Keelogues.htm

Killaraght

- Killaraght Cemetery, Boyle, County Sligo, Ireland
  www.interment.net/data/ireland/sligo/killaraght/killaraght.htm

Kilmacowen

- Kilmacowen
  homepage.eircom.net/%7Ekevm/kilmacowen/kilmacowen/htm
  List of inscriptions

Lisadell

- Lisadell Church, Co. Sligo
  homepage.eircom.net/%7Ekevm/Lisadell/Lisadell.htm
  Photographs of headstones

Rathcormack

- Rathcormack
  homepage.eircom.net/%7Ekevm/Rathcormack/Rathcormack.htm
  List of inscriptions

Rosses Point

- Rosses Point Cemetery
  homepage.eircom.net/%7Ekevm/Rosses__PointIntro.htm
  List of inscriptions

Saint Columba
- Saint Columbas Cemetery, County Sligo, Ireland
  www.interment.net/data/ireland/sligo/stcolumbas.htm

Saint Joseph
- Saint Joseph Cemetery, County Sligo, Ireland
  www.interment.net/data/ireland/sligo/stjoseph/joseph.htm

Scarden
- Scarden
  homepage.eircom.net/%7Ekevm/Ahamlish/Scarden/Intro.htm
  List of inscriptions

Sooey
- Sooey
  homepage.eircom.net/%7Ekevm/Sooey/Sooey.htm
  List of inscriptions at Ballinakill Cemetery

Templeboy
- [Templeboy Cemeteries]
  www.puregolduk.com/bren/MI's%20Co.%20Sligo.htm

- Tombstones at Corcagh Cemetery, Templeboy Parish
  www.rootsweb.com/~irlsli/cemetery4.html
  Surnames only

Templeronan
- Templeronan Cemetery, County Sligo, Ireland
  www.interment.net/data/ireland/sligo/templeronan/templeronan.htm

Thurlestrane
- Thurlestrane
  homepage.eircom.net/%7Ekevm/Thurlestrane/thurlestrane.htm
  Inscriptions

- St. Attracta's, Thurlestrane: Stained Glass Windows
  homepage.eircom.net/~kevm/Thurlestrane/thurlestrane.htm
  Inscriptions

Tipperary
Ardcrony
- Some Memorials to the Dead: Ardcrony Churchyard
  www.rootsweb.com/~irltip2/

Bansha
- Bansha: Bansha Parish
  www.geocities.com/luanndevries/Bansha.html

Cahir
- Cahir: Old Church
  www.geocities.com/luanndevries/CAHIR.html

Clogheen
- Castlegrace Graveyard, Clogheen, County Tipperary
  www.geocities.com/luanndevries/CASTLEGRACE.html

Clonmel
- Marlfield, Clonmel Parish
  www.geocities.com/luanndevries/Marlfield.html
- Saint Patrick Cemetery, Clonmel, County Tipperary, Ireland
  www.interment.net/data/ireland/tipperary/stpatrick/patrick.htm

Dovea
- Irish Cemeteries: Dovea, Old Glendermott, Ileigh, Inch Old Cemetery
  members.iinet.net.au/~sgrieves/cemeteries__ireland__2.htm
  Inscriptions. Old Glendermott is in Londonderry

Fethard
- Augustinian Abbey Cemetery, Fethard, County Tipperary, Ireland
  www.interment.net/data/ireland/tipperary/augustinian__abbey/
                                                    august.htm

Ileigh
See Dovea

Inch
See Dovea

Kilcommon
- Kilcommon: Protestant
  www.geocities.com/luanndevries/KILCOMMON-PROT.html

- Kilcommon: Quaker
  www.geocities.com/luanndevries/KILCOMMON-QUAKER.html

Killadriffe
- Killadriffe Headstone Inscriptions (partial)
  www.rootsweb.com/~irltip2/kiladriffe.htm

Killardry
- Some Memorials to the Dead in County Tipperary: Killardry Churchyard
  www.rootsweb.com/~irltip2/killardry.htm

Lorrha
- Lorrha Cemetery, County Tipperary, Ireland
  www.interment.net/data/ireland/tipperary/lorrha/

Littleton
- Ballymureen Graveyard, Littleton, Co.Tipperary
  www.otherdays.com/presentation/asp/search/
  presAffOther.asp?dbid=132

  Pay per view database

Loughloher
- Loughloher (graveyard and church in ruins)
  www.geocities.com/luanndevries/LOUGHLOHER01.html
  Inscriptions

Loughmore
- Cemetery Headstone Inscriptions Ireland: Loughmore Catholic Cemetery
  members.iinet.net.au/~sgrieves/cemetriesireland3.htm

Roscrea
- Saint Cronan Church of Ireland Churchyard, Roscrea, County Tipperary, Ireland
  www.interment.net/data/ireland/tipperary/stcronan/

Shanrahan
- Shanrahan Graveyard
  www.geocities.com/luanndevries/SHANRAHAN.html

Tyrone
- County Tyrone Cemetery Index
  www.rootsweb.com/~nirtyr3/Cemetery/cemetery.html
  Includes inscriptions from various cemeteries

Clonoe
- Brockagh Graveyard, Clonoe, County Tyrone
  www.otherdays.com/presentation/asp/search/
  presAffOther.asp?dbid=138

  Pay per view database

- Gravestone Inscriptions, Saint Michael's, Clonoe
  www.from-ireland.net/graves/clonoetyrone.htm

- Clonoe Graveyard, County Tyrone
  www.otherdays.com/presentation/asp/search/
  presAffOther.asp?dbid=139

  Pay per view database

Coalisland
- Coalisland Graveyard, County Tyrone
  www.otherdays.com/presentation/asp/search/
  presAffOther.asp?dbid=140

  Pay per view database

Glenhoy
- Glenhoy Presbyterian Church
  freepages.genealogy.rootsweb.com/~cotyroneireland/
  churchrecord/glenhoy.html

Killeeshil
- Killeeshil Chapel
  www.rootsweb.com/~nirtyr3/Cemetery/Killeeshil2.htm

Waterford

Drumcannon
- Tallow Churchyard; Whitechurch Churchyard; Drumcannon
  www.rootsweb.com/~irlwat2/talmem.htm

Dunhill

- Dunhill Churchyard
  www.rootsweb.com/~irlwat2/dunmem.htm

Dunmore East

- Killea Church, Dunmore East, Co. Waterford
  homepage.eircom.net/%7Ekevm/Killea/Killea.htm
  List of monuments

Kilmacow

- St. Senans Cemetery, Kilmacow
  www.from-ireland.net/graves/senanskilmacowwat.htm
  Inscriptions

Lismore

- Lismore: St. Carthagh's Cathedral
  www.rootsweb.com/~irlwat2/lismmem.htm
  Survey of inscriptions

Westmeath

Castlepollard

- Killafree Cemetery, Castlepollard, County Westmeath, Ireland
  www.interment.net/data/ireland/westmeath/killafree/killafree.htm

Delvin

- Headstones in St. Mary's Churchyard, Delvin, Co. Westmeath
  www.from-ireland.net/graves/delvinwestmeath.htm

Finea

- Castletown Churchyard, Finea, County Westmeath, Ireland
  www.interment.net/data/ireland/westmeath/castletown/

Fore

- St. Feichin Churchyard, New Cemetery, Fore, County Westmeath, Ireland
  www.interment.net/data/ireland/westmeath/newfechin.htm

- Saint Feichin Old Cemetery, Fore, County Westmeath
  www.interment.net/data/ireland/westmeath/oldfechin/fechins.htm

Mullingar

- Turin Cemetery, Mullingar, County Westmeath, Ireland
  www.interment.net/data/ireland/westmeath/turin/turin.htm

Wexford

- Graveyards & Churches in Co. Wexford
  www.from-ireland.net/graves/wexchugraves.htm
  List

- Wexford Gravestones: Place Name Index
  www.from-ireland.net/graves/wex/placenames.htm

Ambrosetown

- Wexford Gravestones: Name Index: Ambrosetown
  www.from-ireland.net/graves/ambrosewex.htm

Ardamine

- Ardamine Graveyard
  www.from-ireland.net/graves/ardaminewexford.htm

Wicklow

Arklow

- St. Mary's Graveyard: Arklow, Co. Wicklow
  www.rootsweb.com/~irlwic2/
  Click on title

Ashford

- Wicklow Gravestones Name Index: Church of the Holy Rosary, Ashford, Co. Wicklow
  www.from-ireland.net/graves/wicklow/holyrosaryashford.htm
  Brief

Askamore

- Askamore Graveyard, Co. Wexford
  www.from-ireland.net/graves/askamorewexford.htm
  Inscriptions

Ballymitty

- Wexford Gravestones: Name Index: Ballymitty St. Peter's R.C. Church
  www.from-ireland.net/graves/ballymittywexford.htm

Bannow

- Wexford Gravestones Name Index: Bannow
  www.from-ireland.net/graves/bannowwex.htm

Barntown

- Wexford Gravestones Name Index: Barntown
  www.from-ireland.net/graves/barntownwex.htm

Ballymagaret

- Wexford Gravestones Name Index: St. Mary's R.C. Church,
  Ballymagaret, Co. Wexford, Ireland
  www.from-ireland.net/graves/wex/bgarrett.htm

Bunclody

- Saint Mary C. of I. Churchyard, Bunclody, County Wexford, Ireland
  www.interment.net/data/ireland/wexford/stmary/

Calvary

- Calvary Cemetery, County Wexford, Ireland
  www.interment.net/data/ireland/wexford/calvary/calvary.htm

Cleristown

- Wexford Gravestones Name Index: Cleriestown (Cleristown) St.
  Mannan's R.C. Church
  www.from-ireland.net/graves/cleriestownwex.htm

Donaghmore

- Donaghmore Old Graveyard
  www.from-ireland.net/graves/donaghmoreoldwex.htm

Hook

- Hook Church Cemetery, County Wexford, Ireland
  www.interment.net/data/ireland/wexford/hook/hook.htm

Kilcavan

- Wexford Graestones Name Index: Kilcavan
  www.from-ireland.net/graves/kilcavan.htm

Kilgorman

- Wexford Gravestones Name Index: Kilgorman
  www.from-ireland.net/graves/wex/kilgorman.htm

Kilmore

- Old Grange Cemetery, Kilmore, County Wexford, Ireland
  www.interment.net/data/ireland/wexford/oldgrange/grange.htm

Kilmyshall

- Wexford Gravestones Name Index: Kilmyshall, Old
  www.from-ireland.net/graves/wex/kilmyshallold.htm

- Wexford Gravestones Name Index: Kilmyshall, R.C.
  www.from-ireland.net/graves/wex/Kilmyshallrc.htm

Kilnahue

- Wexford Gravestones: Kilnahue old (near Gorey), Wexford, Ireland
  www.from-ireland.net/graves/wex/kilnahnueold.htm
  Name index

Kilrush

- Wexford Gravestones Name Index: Kilrush, Church of Ireland
  Graveyard, Co. Wexford, Ireland
  www.from-ireland.net/graves/wex/kilrushcoi.htm
  Name index

- Wexford Gravestones Name Index: Kilrush, Roman Catholic, Ireland
  www.from-ireland.net/graves/wex/kilrushc.htm

- Kilrush R.C.
  www.from-ireland.net/graves/kilrushwexford.htm
  List of surnames from inscriptions

Kiltennel

- Kiltennel Graveyard, St. Sinchell, Church of Ireland
  www.from-ireland.net/graves/kiltennellwexford.htm

Knockbrandon

- Wexford Gravestones Name Index: Knockbrandon Old, Wexford, Ireland
  www.from-ireland.net/graves/wex/knockbrandonld.htm

Leskinfere

- Wexford Gravestones Name Index: Leskinfere, St. Lukes, Church of Ireland, Ireland
  www.from-ireland.net/graves/wex/leskinfere.htm

Monaseed

- Wexford Gravestones Name Index: Monaseed Roman Catholic Graveyard, Ireland
  www.from-ireland.net/graves/wex/monaseedrc.htm

Prospect

- Wexford Gravestones Name Index: Prospect Church of Ireland Graveyard, Ireland
  www.from-ireland.net/graves/wex/prospectcoi.htm

Taghmon

- Wexford Gravestones Name Index: St. Mannas, Taghmon, Wexford, Ireland
  www.from-ireland.net/graves/wex/taghmannas.htm

Templeshanbo

- Templeshanbo Old
  www.from-ireland.net/graves/templeshwex.htm
  Some inscriptions, with list of surnames from others

Templetown

- Templetown Cemetery, County Wexford, Ireland
  www.interment.net/data/ireland/wexford/templeton/temple.htm

Wicklow

Arklow

- County Wickow, Arklow Parish: St. Gabriel's, Arklow, Barinsky Gravestone Inscriptions (or death records)
  www.cmcrp.net/Wicklow/stgabcem.htm

Baltinglass

- Baltinglass Cemetery, County Wicklow, Ireland
  www.interment.net/data/ireland/wicklow/baltinglass/baltinglass.htm

- Saint Mary Abbey Churchyard, Baltinglass, County Wicklow, Ireland
  www.interment.net/data/ireland/wicklow/stmary/

Bray

- Wicklow Gravestones Name Index: Church of the Most Holy Redeemer, Bray, Co. Wicklow
  www.from-ireland.net/graves/wicklow/holyredeembray.htm

- Wicklow Gravestones Name Index: Bray Little Graveyard (St. Peter's Chapel)
  www.from-ireland.net/graves/wicklow/littlebray.htm

Davistown

- Davistown Cemetery, Davistown, County Wicklow, Ireland
  www.interment.net/data/ireland/wicklow/davistown/davis.htm

Delgany

- Wicklow Gravestones Name Index: Delgany, old
  www.from-ireland.net/graves/wicklow/delganyold.htm

Derralossary

- Wicklow Gravestones Name Index: Derralossary
  www.from-ireland.net/graves/wicklow/derralossary.htm

Dunlavin

- Dunlavin Cemetery, Dunlavin, County Wicklow, Ireland
  www.interment.net/data/ireland/wicklow/dunlavin/dunlavin.htm

Glendalough
- Saint Kevin Cemetery, Glendalough, County Wicklow, Ireland
  www.interment.net/data/ireland/wicklow/stkev__glen/

Heighington
- Heighington Burial Ground, County Wicklow, Ireland
  www.interment.net/data/ireland/wicklow/heighington/heighington.htm

Killoughter
- Wicklow Gravestones Name Index: Killoughter
  www.from-ireland.net/graves/killoughter.htm

Kilquade
- Wicklow Gravestones Name Index: Kilquade
  www.from-ireland.net/graves/kilquade.htm

Kilmacanogue
- Wicklow Gravestones Name Index: Kilmacanogue.htm
  www.from-ireland.net/graves/kilmacanogue.htm

Kilranalagh
- Kilranalagh Graveyard, County Wicklow, Ireland
  www.interment.net/data/ireland/wicklow/kilranalagh/kilranalagh.htm

Leitrim
- Leitrim Cemetery, County Wicklow, Ireland
  www.interment.net/data/ireland/wicklow/leitrim/

Powerscourt
- Wicklow Gravestones Name Index: Powerscourt Demesne (Churchtown)
  www.from-ireland.net/graves/wicklow/powerscourtdem.htm

Roundwood
- Wicklow Gravestones Name Index: Roundwood, St. Laurence O'Toole, R.C.
  www.from-ireland/net/graves/wicklow/roundwoodstlaur.htm

Saint Kevins
- Saint Kevin's Churchyard Cemetery, County Wicklow, Ireland
  www.interment.net/data/ireland/wicklow/stkevin/kevin.htm

Saint Nicholas
- Saint Nicholas Cemetery, County Wicklow, Ireland
  www.interment.net/data/ireland/wicklow/nicholas/nicholas.htm

Trinity
- Wicklow Gravestones Name Index: Trinity
  www.from-ireland.net/graves/wicklow/trinity.htm

Tyneclash
- Tyneclash Old Cemetery County Wicklow, Ireland
  www.interment.net/data/ireland/wicklow/tyneclash/tyneclash.htm

11. Other Sources

Information on a wide range of sources is available on the net. This includes much valuable advice; it also includes many sites providing the actual data. A wide variety of sources have sites devoted to them; these are listed here, prefaced by a listing of sites with database and source collections.

- ≈ DIGdat: Digital Irish Genealogy Data
  www.ajmorris.com/dig/
  Pay per view site, but with some free data, and also many fiche offered for sale

- Family History: computerised family history databases
  ireland.iol.ie/irishworld/famhist.htm
  Fee-based list of searchable databases (the databases themselves are not on-line)

- Irish Family Research
  www.irishfamilyresearch.co.uk
  Collection of c.70 databases, including Griffith's Valuation, trade directories, educational records, *etc.* Pay per view site

- Irish Origins
  www.irishorigins.com
  Small collection of databases, including the important Griffith's Valuation

- Irish Records Extraction Database
  www.ancestry.com/search/rectype/inddbs/3876a.htm
  c.100,000 records from 100 different sources - but little indication of what the sources are

- Irish Source Records 1500s-1800s
  www.genealogy.com/275facd.html
  Subscription based index to a wide variety of sources: census, return of owners of land. Griffiths, wills, *etc.*

- A little bit of Ireland
  www.celticcousins.net/ireland/
  Mainly transcriptions of original sources

- Otherdays.com: Irish Genealogy
  www.otherdays.com
  Collection of databases; pay per view

- U.K. & Ireland Records
  **www.ancestry.com/Landing/product/search/
  uki.aspx?html=uki2&o__xid=0033089833&o__lid=0033089833**
  Collection of databases - but no information on what they are and what relates to Ireland

- Casey Bibliography: the mother lode of Irish Genealogy
  www.rootsweb.com/~irish/igsi__published/casey.htm
  Detailed description of a genealogist's collection of notes on 3,000,000 names

Admiralty Examinations

- High Court of Admiralty Examinations, 1536-1641: material relating to Ireland
  www.from-ireland.net/history/admirindex/admirintrolinks.htm
  Surname index

Business Records

- Business Records Survey
  **www.nationalarchives.ie/cgi-bin/
  naigenform02?index=Business+Records+Survey**

- Business Records
  proni.nics.gov.uk/records/business.htm
  In the Public Record Office of Northern Ireland

- The Harland & Wolff Archive
  proni.nics.gov.uk/records/private/harwolf.htm
  Description of business records of the ship builders; including staff records

Catholic Qualification Rolls

Donegal

- Catholic Qualification Rolls 1778-1790. Donegal
  www.ulsterancestry.com/
  ua-free-Donegal__Catholic__Qualification__Rolls.html

Fermanagh

- Catholic Qualifation Rolls Index: Fermanagh
  www.from-ireland.net/gene/fermanaghcathqualrolls.htm

Galway

- The Catholic Convert Rolls
  www.from-ireland.net/gene/convertrolls.htm
  Includes list of names from Galway

Monaghan

- Catholic Qualification Rolls. County Monaghan c.1778
  www.ulsterancestry.com/ua-free__MonaghanQualificationRolls1778.html

- Catholic Qualification Rolls Index: County Monaghan, c.1778
  ahd.exis.net/monaghan/qual-cath.htm

Census

- Actual Censuses
  www.rootsweb.com/~fianna/guide/cen1.html
  Details of availability of the 1901 and 1911 censuses, and of fragments
  from previous censuses

- Census Links for Ireland
  www.censusfinder.com/ireland.htm
  Gateway; also includes links to sites with trade directories, Griffith's
  Valuation, baptism registers, *etc.*

- Census Records
  scripts.ireland.com/ancestor/browse/records/census
  Introduction

- Censuses
  www.rootsweb.com/~fianna/guide/census.html/
  Overview of Irish censuses and census substitutes

- Census Returns
  freepages.genealogy.rootsweb.com/~irishancestors/
  Census%20returns.html
  Introduction

- Census Returns
  www.nationalarchives.ie/censusrtns.html
  From the National Archives

- Ireland Census Records
  www.censusfinder.com/ireland.htm
  Lists census records online

- Irish Census Records
  www.scotlandsclans.com/ircensus.htm

- Irish Census Returns at the National Archives in Dublin
  www.genealogy.ie/categories/cenna/

- Online Irish Census Indexes & Records: Ireland Census Records by
  County: a genealogy guide
  www.genealogybranches.com/irishcensus.html

- Scots and Irish Strays Census Indexes
  rontay.digiweb.com/scot/
  This website no longer exists, but an archive copy can be found at
  web.archive.org/web/web.php

- Seventeenth Century Census Substitutes
  scripts.ireland.com/ancestor/browse/records/census/seven.htm

- Seventeenth Century Census Substitutes
  proni.nics.gov.uk/records/17cent.htm

- Census Substitutes 18th and 19th Century
  proni.nics.gov.uk/records/census.htm
  Lists various sources giving census-like information

- Eighteenth & Nineteenth Century Census Substitutes
  scripts.ireland.com/ancestor/browse/records/census/eight.htm

- Census Records: 19th Century
  proni.nics.gov.uk/census19.htm

- 1901 Census
  proni.nics.gov.uk/records/1901cens.htm

Antrim

- Antrim Agricultural Census 1803
  www.otherdays.com/presentation/asp/search/
  presAffOther.asp?dbid=108

  Pay per view database

- [1851 Co. Antrim Census]
  irishgenealogy.net/TOWNLANDS.html

- 1901 Census Extracts, County Antrim, Ireland: Belfast: Balmoral
  Industrial School
  www.from-ireland.net/censusabstracts/ant/1901/belfast/balmoral.htm

Armagh

- McConville's Irish Genealogy: the first census of the Fews, 1602
  www.mcconville.org/main/genealogy/census1602.html
  The Fews is a barony in Armagh

Cavan

- C.M.C.
  cmcrp.net/Othercty/Cavan1821-1.htm
  Extracts from the 1821 census for Co. Cavan

Clare See also Limerick

- 1901 Census of County Clare
  www.clarelibrary.ie/eolas/coclare/genealogy/
  1901census/1901__clare__census.htm

- 1901 Census Index, County Clare
  www.connorsgenealogy.com/clare/clarecensuspage.html
  For the Poor Law Unions of Ennistimon, Kildysart and Kilmaley

Cork

- 1911 Census: County Cork
  www.rootsweb.com/~fianna/county/cor1911.html
  List of films at the Family History Library

- 1851 census for Kilcrumper, Kilworth, Leitrim, and Macroney: excerpts
  www.ginnisw.com/1851%20Census%20in%20Excel.htm

Donegal

- Census Records
  freepages.genealogy.rootsweb.com/~donegal/census.htm
  For many places, mainly 1901 and 1911

- Names of Protestant Householders in the year 1766 in the Parish of
  Leck, Barony of Raphoe, Co.Donegal, Ireland
  freepages.genealogy.rootsweb.com/~donegal/leck1766.htm

Galway
  See Leitrim

Kerry

- 1659 Census, County Kerry, Ireland
  www.rootsweb.com/~irlker/census16a.html
  Pender census

- 1901 census
  www.rootsweb.com/~irlker/census.html
  Co.Kerry; incomplete

- 1901 Census: County Kerry
  www.rootsweb.com/~irlker/census01cp.html

- 1911 Census: County Kerry
  www.rootsweb.com/~irlker/census11.html

- A Census of the Parishes of Prior and Killemlagh, December 1834
  www.rootsweb.com/~irlker/1834text.html

Kildare
- Kildare Heritage & Genealogy Co. 1901 census
  kildare.ie/library/KildareHeritage/Census.htm
  List of computerised 1901 census returns

Leitrim
- Leitrim-Roscommon 1901 Census Home Page
  www.leitrim-roscommon.com/1901census/
  Covers Galway, Leitrim, Mayo, Roscommon, Sligo and Westmeath

Limerick
- 1901 Census of Ireland
  home.att.net/~bristolman/1901__census.htm
  Information from townlands in Co. Limerick and Co. Clare

Londonderry
- 1831 census: Dunboe Parish, Co. Londonderry
  www.rootsweb.com/~nirldy/dunboe/1831cen/1831indx.htm

Longford
- 1901 Census Returns for the Parish of Edgeworthstown
  www.mostrim.org/Scrapbook/Words/census1.htm

Mayo *See also* Leitrim
- Census and Heads of Households, Co. Mayo, Ireland, 1901 and 1911
  freepages.genealogy.rootsweb.com/~deesegenes/cen.html
  Many pages for various parishes
- 1901 census for County Mayo, Ireland: East Mayo
  www.rootsweb.com/~fianna/county/mayo/emay1901.html
- 1901 Census for the Parish of Burrishoole
  www.geocities.com/Heartland/Park/7461/cens.html

Meath
- 1901 County Meath Census
  www.angelfire.com/ak2/ashbourne/townlandlist.html

Roscommon
  See Leitrim

Sligo *See also* Leitrim
- Sligo County, Ireland, 1901 Census
  www.rootsweb.com/irlsli/index2.html

Tipperary
- 1821 Census Fragments, Co. Tipperary
  www.rootsweb.com/~irltip2/census__1821.htm
- 1901 Census Extracts
  www.rootsweb.com/~irltip2/Census/
  For Co. Tipperary

Westmeath
  See Roscommon

Church of Ireland
- The Church of Ireland: genealogy and family history
  www.ireland.anglican.org/library/libroots.html
  Notes on parish registers and other sources
- Church of Ireland Index
  proni.nics.gov.uk/records/private/cofiindx.htm
  Records at the Public Record Office of Northern Ireland
- Church of Ireland Vestry Records
  proni.nics.gov.uk/records/vestry.htm
  Brief note
- The Armagh Diocesan Registry Archive
  proni.nics.gov.uk/records/private/armagh.htm
  General discussion, 13-20th c.

Louth

- Tullyallen New Church
  www.rootsweb.com/~fianna/county/louth/loutchu.html
  List of subscribers 1898

Meath

- Protestant Parishioners: Diocese of Meath 1802
  www.from-ireland.net/censussubs/meath1802.htm
  Index to a list of names returned following a bishop's enquiry

Church Records

- Church Records
  proni.nics.gov.uk/records/church.htm
  In the Public Record Office of Northern Ireland; includes those of various denominations

- Clogher Diocesan Records: Roman Catholic and Church of Ireland
  proni.nics.gov.uk/records/private/clogher.htm

Confirmation Records

- Ginni Swanton's Web Site Confirmation Records, parishes of Enniskeane, Desertserges and Kinneigh, County Cork
  www.ginnisw.com/confirma1.htm

Deeds

- Registry of Deeds
  www.irlgov.ie/landreg/default.htm
  The registry is able to supply memorials of deeds from 1708

- Registry of Deeds
  scripts.ireland.com/ancestor/browse/records/deeds/

- Registry of Deeds
  proni.nics.gov.uk/records/deeds.htm
  For Northern Ireland

Cavan

- Deeds on L.D.S. Film
  www.sierratel.com/colinf/genuki/CAV/Deeds/
  For Co. Cavan, from the Registry of Deeds

Fermanagh

- Fermanagh Deeds (also known as the Brooke deeds)
  www.ulsterancestry.com/ua-BrookeDeeds.html
  18-20th c.

Diaries

- The Harshaw Diaries
  proni.nics.gov.uk/records/private/harshaw.htm
  Description of the diaries of James Harshaw of Donaghmore, mid 19th c. They contain much information on local baptisms, marriages and burials

Directories

- Directories
  scripts.ireland.com/ancestor/browse/records/directories
  General introduction

- Directories
  www.iol.ie/dublincitylibrary/gadirectories.htm
  In Dublin City Library

- Pigot's Provincial Directory of Ireland 1824
  members.cox.net/hayes1966/pigot.htm

- Slaters Commercial Directory of Ireland 1846
  members.cox.net/hayes1966/slater.htm

Antrim

- Antrim Directory 1849
  www.otherdays.com/presentation/asp/search/
  presAffOther.asp?dbid=226

- Bassetts County Antrim 1888 Directory
  www.ajmorris.com/dig/toc/__01dant.htm
  Pay per view site

Carlow
  See also Cork and Waterford

Clare

- Francis Guy's directory of Munster 1886: Ardnacrusha, Co. Clare
  home.att.net/~labaths/ardna.htm

- Clonlara, Co. Clare, 1886
  home.att.net/~labaths/clonlara.htm
  Directory entries

- A general directory of the Kingdom of Ireland 1788: Ennis, County of Clare
  home.att.net/~labaths/1788dire.htm

- Slaters Directory of Ireland 1856: Ennis
  home.att.net/~labaths/1856dire.htm

Cork

- Pigott's Directory 1824 (South East)
  www.otherdays.com/presentation/asp/search/
  presAffOther.asp?dbid=128
  Pay per view database; covers Co's Cork, Tipperary, Waterford, and Wexford

- Slater's Directory 1846 (South East Ireland)
  www.otherdays.com/presentation/asp/search/
  presAffOther.asp?dbid=105
  Pay per view database

- Slater's Directory 1856 (South East Ireland)
  www.otherdays.com/presentation/asp/search/
  presAffOther.asp?dbid=109
  Pay per view database; covers Carlow, Cork, Kilkenny, Tipperary, Waterford, Wexford and Wicklow

- Slater's Directory 1881 (South East Ireland)
  www.otherdays.com/presentation/asp/search/presAffOther.asp?dbid=110
  Pay per view database; covers Carlow, Cork, Kilkenny, Tipperary, Waterford, Wexford and Wicklow

- Ginni Swanton's Web Site: Francis Guy's County and City of Cork Directory for the years 1875-1876.
  www.ginnisw.com/
  Excludes Cork City

- Henry & Coghlan's General Directory of Cork for 1867
  homepage.eircom.net/~ridgway/1867Corkcitydirectory.htm

- Guys Postal Directory 1914 for County Cork, Ireland
  members.cox.net/hayes1966/guy.htm

Donegal

- 1824 Pigot's Directory, Donegal
  freepages.genealogy.rootsweb.com/~donegal/1824pigots.htm

- 1846 Slater's Directory, Donegal
  freepages.genealogy.rootsweb.com/~donegal/1846dir.txt

- Notes on Donegal towns: Ballybofey, Ballyshannon, & Donegal Town (from *Slaters Directory* 1857)
  freepages.genealogy.rootsweb.com/~donegal/1857dir.htm

Dublin

- Pettigrew and Oulton's Dublin Directory 1838
  www.ajmorris.com/dig/toc/__01du38.htm
  Pay per view site

- Shaw's Dublin City Directory 1850
  www.loughman.dna.ie/dublin1850

Fermanagh

- Ireland, County Fermanagh Directory and Household Almanac 1880
  www.ajmorris.com/dig/toc/__01ferm.htm
  Pay per view site

Kilkenny See also Cork and Waterford

- Egan's Kilkenny Directory 1884
  www.otherdays.com/presentation/asp/search/
  presAffOther.asp?dbid=137
  Pay per view database

- The Kilkenny City & County Directory 1884
  www.otherdays.com/presentation/asp/search/presAffOther.asp?dbid=115
  Pay per view database

Limerick

- A General Directory of the Kingdom of Ireland 1788: Limerick
  home.att.net/~labaths/lim1788.txt

- Ferrar's Limerick Directory of 1769
  home.att.net/~labaths/lim.htm
  City

- Limerick City Directory 1788: an extract from the General directory of the Kingdom of Ireland, 1788
  www.geocities.com/irishancestralpages/limdir1788main.html

- A General Directory of the Kingdom of Ireland 1788: Limerick
  home.att.net/~labaths/lim1788.htm

Longford

- Longford Town Directory 1894
  www.rootsweb.com/~irllog/directory.htm

Mayo

- Slater's Directory 1846
  www.geocities.com/Heartland/Park/7461/unindslat.html
  For Burrishoole, Co. Mayo

- Business in Castlebar 1824
  freepages.genealogy.rootsweb.com/~deesegenes/cbb.html
  From a Co. Mayo directory

- Castlebar, Co. Mayo, Ireland Directory 1846 incomplete
  freepages.genealogy.rootsweb.com/~deesegenes/cas.html

- Westport, Co. Mayo, Ireland Directory 1846 incomplete
  freepages.genealogy.rootsweb.com/deesegenes/west.html

Tipperary *See also* Cork

- The Book of County Tipperary: a manual and directory ... 1889
  www.rootsweb.com/~irltip2/directory/bassetts.html

- Pigots Directory of Ireland 1824
  www.rootsweb.com/~irltip2/pigotndx.htm
  Extracts for Co. Tipperary

- Slaters Directory of Ireland, 1856
  www.rootsweb.com/~irltip2/slatersndx.htm
  Extracts for Co. Tipperary

Waterford *See also* Cork

- Shearman's New Commercial Directory 1839
  www.otherdays.com/presentation/asp/search/
  presAffOther.asp?dbid=130
  Pay per view database, covers Co's Waterford, Kilkenny and Carlow

- Henry and Coughlan's Directory 1867 (Waterford)
  www.otherdays.com/presentation/asp/search/
  presAffOther.asp?dbid=175
  Pay per view database

- Egan's Waterford Directory 1894
  www.otherdays.com/presentation/asp/search/
  presAffOther.asp?dbid=142
  Pay per view database

- Thom's Directory for Waterford 1909-1910
  www.otherdays.com/presentation/asp/search/
  presAffOther.asp?dbid=156
  Pay per view database

- Waterford Almanac and Street Directory 1877
  www.otherdays.com/presentation/asp/search/
  presAffOther.asp?dbid=136
  Pay per view database; covers the city only.

Wexford See also Cork

- Wexford County Directory & Guide 1885
  www.otherdays.com/presentation/asp/search/
  presAffOther.asp?dbid=122

  Pay per view database

Ejectment Books
- Surviving Ejectment Books
  www.rootsweb.com/~irlcla/landejectlist.html
  For Co. Clare 1816-1914. General description of a source that lists tenants threatened with eviction.

Electoral Registers & Records
- Marksmen (Illiterate Voters) Belfast 1837
  www.otherdays.com/presentation/asp/search/
  presAffOther.asp?dbid=204

  Pay per view database

- 1926 Register of Electors Killarney
  www.rootsweb.com/~irlker/elkill1.html

- Voters: Poll and Freeholders Records
  proni.nics.gov.uk/records/voters.htm
  List of records for Ulster

Emigrant Savings Bank
- A Users Guide to the Emigrant Bank Records
  www.nypl.org/research/chss/spe/rbk/faids/emigrant.html
  The Bank was founded by the Irish Emigrant Society for the Irish in New York

Emigration
There are numerous sites devoted to emigration - especially those giving passenger lists. Sites which deal with just one journey are not listed here as there are far too many. For general introductions, see:
- Exodus
  www.belfasttelegraph.co.uk/emigration/
  Archived at **web.archive.org/web/web.php**

- Introduction to Passenger List Research
  www.rootsweb.com/~fianna/migrate/pass.html

- Emigration Records
  proni.nics.gov.uk/records/emigrate.htm
  In the Public Record Office of Northern Ireland

See also:
- Famine and Emigration Links
  freepages.genealogy.rootsweb.com/~irishancestors/Famine.html

Books, CDs, *etc.,* are vital resources, and are listed at:
- Emigration
  scripts.ireland.com/ancestor/browse/emigration/index.htm
  Bibliographical guide

- Irish Passenger Lists Research Guide: Finding Ship Passenger & Immigration Records, Ireland to America: a bibliography of books, CD-Roms, Microfilm, & Online Records
  www.genealogybranches.com/irishpassengerlists/

- Passenger Lists and Immigration 1700-1800
  www.rootsweb.com/~fianna/migrate/passearly.html
  Book list for U.S. and North American migration

A number of institutions have useful sites
- Centre for Migration Studies at the Ulster American Folk Park
  www.qub.ac.uk/cms/

- Irish Migration Resource Center
  www.irishmigration.com/
  Archived at **web.archive.org/web/web.php**

- Immigrant Ships Transcribers Guild
  www.immigrantships.net/
  Transcripts of passenger lists from many ships

For records held by the Latter Day Saints, see:
- L.D.S. Records on Irish Migration
  www.rootsweb.com/~fianna/migrate/ldse.html

Other sites with links to passenger lists include:
- Ancestor Search: Ship Passenger Lists Search Engine
  www.searchforancestors.com/records/passenger.html
  International scope, but much of Irish interest

- Dunbrody: Ireland's Historic Emigrant Ship: Emigration Database
  www.dunbrody.com/home.htm
  Click on 'Emigrants Database'. Brief description of an important off-line database.

- Emigrants from Ireland
  www.ajmorris.com/dig/fap/rec/
  Registration needed. Click on title. Transcripts of passenger lists

- Famine: Irish Passenger Record Datafile
  aad.archives.gov/aad/
                  file__unit__description.jsp?file__id=640&coll__id-1002

- Irish Passenger Lists
  members.tripod.com/~Data__Mate/irish/Irish.htm
  Numerous transcripts

- Irish Passenger Lists
  members.tripod.com/~Data__Mate/irish/Irish.htm
  List of lists

- Passenger Lists
  scripts.ireland.com/ancestor/browse/links/passdatepre1800.htm

- Passenger Lists arranged by County and Destination
  www.rootsweb.com/~fianna/migrate/shiplists.html
  Comprehensive gateway for Irish lists

- Search Engines for Ships From Ireland
  olivetreegenealogy.com/ships/searchirish.shtml

- Sites with Genealogical Source Material: Irish Passenger Lists
  freespace.virgin.net/alan.tupman/sites/irish.htm
  Numerous lists, mainly 19th c.

For emigration to specific places see:

Argentina
- 19th Century: Irish Emigration to Argentina
  www.ite.ie/nua/argentina.pdf
  www.islandeses.com.ar
  Lecture

Australia
- The Female Irish (potato famine) orphans: girls to Sydney, Melbourne and Adelaide
  users/bigpond.net.au/convicts/page3.html
  Combined passenger lists, 1848-50

Canada
- Immigrants to Canada
  ist.uwaterloo.ca/~marj/genealogy/thevoyage.html
  General introduction with many links

- Immigration/Migration Records: Atlantic Provinces, Canada
  www.rootsweb.com/~fianna/oc/canada/can-nb.html

- Immigration Records
  www.archives.ca/02/02020204__e.html
  In the National Archives of Canada

- Grosse-île in Quebec: the last resting place for over 6,000 Irish souls
  www.moytura.com/grosse-ile.htm
  General discussion; no names

- Grosse-île and the Irish Memorial: National Historic Site of Canada
  parkscanada.pch.gc.ca/grosseile/
  General description; no names

- West Ireland Emigration to Canada
  www.teamapproach.ca/irish/

- Irish Famine Migration to New Brunswick 1845-1852
  archives.gnb.ca/APPS/PrivRecs/IrishFamine/
  Default-e.aspx?PageLoad=SearchForm

- Prince Edward Island Data Pages: Irish born in PE1 before 1846
  homepages.rootsweb.com/~mvreid/pei/peirish.html

New Zealand
- The Irish in New Zealand
  www.mch.govt.nz/ref/enz/irish/

- List of New Zealand Irish Migrants
  www.geocities.com/nziconnection/immlist.htm

- N.Z. - Ireland Connection
  www.geocities.com/Heartland/Prairie/7271/

United States
- Irish Immigrants
  www.cimorelli.com/ireland/selectirish.htm
  See also **/irishpass.html**
  Database of emigrants to the U.S.A.

- Irish Immigrants to North America 1803-1871
  www.genealogy.com/257facd.html
  Subscription based database, presumably from published sources

- The Irish in America: Irish Genealogy
  www.pbs.org/wgbh/pages/irish/genealogy.html
  Archived at **web.archive.org/web/web.php**
  Brief guide

- Irish to America 1846-1865: passenger and immigration lists
  www.ancestry.com/357facd.html
  Subscription based database, compiled from the original ship manifest schedules. Continued to 1886 at **/264facd.html**

- New England Irish Pioneers
  www.ancestry.com/search/rectype/inddbs/1008.htm
  17th c.

- Olive Tree Genealogy: Irish to America
  olivetreegenealogy.com/ships/irishtousa.shtml
  Includes various databases, fee-based and free

- Ship Passenger Lists from Ireland to America: miscellaneous ships
  www.ancestry.com/search/db/aspx?dbid=6138

- Chicago Irish Families 1875-1925
  www.geocities.com/Heartland/Park/7461/chicago.html

- The Famine Immigrants
  www.lalley.com/
  Click on 'Passengers'. Immigrants to Wilmington, Delaware

- The Irish in Iowa
  www.celticcousins.net/irishiniowa

- Irish Immigration into Maryland
  oriole.umd.edu/~mddlmddl/791/Communities/html/irisha.html
  Article

- The Irish in Nineteenth Century New York and beyond
  freepages.genealogy.rootsweb.com/~nyirish/research.html

- New York - Irish Genealogy
  freepages.genealogy.rootsweb.com/~irishancestors/New York.html
- Irish Quaker Immigration into Pennsylvania
  www.ancestry.com/search/db.aspx?dbid=3300
  Database; pay per view
- The Irish in 19th-century Portsmouth, N.H.
  www.fortunecity.com/bally/limerick/123/ports/dir.htm
- Rhode Island Irish
  www.fortunecity.com/bally/westmeath/278/
- Irish Immigrants to Virginia
  ftp.rootsweb.com/pub/usgenweb/va/misc/irishva.txt
  List, mid-17th c.
- Wilmington, Delaware's Irish roots
  www.lalley.com
  Includes Griffiths valuation,1855, for Annoghdown, Donagh Patrick, Kilcoona, Kilkilvery, Killeany, and Killursa, in Co. Galway; also 1801 census for Cargin, Co Galway

For emigration from specific places see:

Carlow
  See Cavan

Cavan
- Surname Index to Passenger Lists with Cavan Passengers
  www.sierratel.com/colinf/genuki/CAV/Passengers/
- County Cavan - St. Croix; West Indies Bound
  maxpages.com/irishcrucians
  19th c. migration
- Cavan Persons in U.S. Records
  www.sierratel.com/colinf/genuki/CAV/USRecords.html

Donegal
- Assisted Immigrants from Donegal arriving in Lyttleton, New Zealand, 1855-1874
  freepages.genealogy.rootsweb.com/~donegal/donpass.htm
- Donegal to Australia
  freepages.genealogy.rootsweb.com/~donegal/relief.htm
  Emigrant records of the Donegal Relief Fund 1858-62
- Irish to America, departing from Donegal 1848-1851
  freepages.genealogy.rootsweb.com/~donegal/IrishtoAmerica.txt

Galway
- Galway Emigrant Index, 1828-1852
  freepages.genealogy.rootsweb.com/~maddenps/GALWAYEM.htm
  Emigrants to Australia

Kerry
- Lansdowne's Estate in Kenmare Assisted Emigration Plan
  www.rootsweb.com/~irlker/lansdowne.html
- State-Aided Emigration Scheme: Castlemaine
  www.rootsweb.com/~irlker/castlemigr.html

Limerick
- Kilmallock Workhouse Emigration
  home.att.net/~bristolman/kilmallock_workhouse.htm
  1850-51

Roscommon
- Ballykilcline Emigrants
  www.rootsweb.com/~irlros/forced.htm
  1844-52

Sligo
- Ships Sailing from Sligo
  www.rootsweb.com/~irlsli/shipshesli.html

Tipperary

- Tipperary Emigrant Index, 1828 to 1865
  freepages.genealogy.rootsweb.com/~maddenps/TIPPEM5.htm
  Emigrants to Australia

Wexford

- Irish Immigrants from County Wexford: New York Port Arrival Records 1846-1851
  users.rootsweb.com/~irlwex2/wexford__immigrants.html

- I.G.S.I: Emigrants from Wexford and Carlow: 5,500 Emigrants (c.1000 families) to Canada (British North America), 1817 from Wexford and Carlow
  www.rootsweb.com/~irish/igsi__published/misc/wexemig.htm

Enclosure Records

- Reports and Returns Relating to Evictions in the Kilrush Union 1849
  **www.clarelibrary.ie/eolas/coclare/history/
  kr__evictions/kr__evictions__enclosures.htm**
  Numerous pages listing enclosure evictions

Encumbered Estates

- Encumbered Estates
  proni.nics.gov.uk/records/encumb.htm
  Brief note on a source giving tenants' names for many 19th c. estates throughout Ireland

Estate Records

- Irish Estate Records
  www.ancestry.com/library/view/ancmag/1957.asp
  General discussion

- Irish Estate Records
  www.rootsweb.com/~irish/igsi__published/cens-sub/betit.htm
  General discussion

- Irish Land Records
  globalgenealogy.com/globalgazette/gazkb/gazkb68.htm
  Continued at **/gazkb670.htm**

- Landed Estate Records
  proni.nics.gov.uk/records/landed.htm
  In the Public Record Office of Northern Ireland (but not just for Ulster)

- Church Temporalities
  proni.nics.gov.uk/records/private/fin-10.htm
  Discussion of 19th c. estate records of the Church of Ireland

- Records of Private Individuals
  proni.nics.gov.uk/records/private.htm
  List of collections of estate and other private papers in the Public Record Office of Northern Ireland (but covering all Ireland)

Cavan

- Cavan Estate Records
  scripts.ireland.com/ancestor/browse/counties/ulster/cavan6.htm
  List of estate archives

- Estate Records
  www.irelandgenweb.com/~cavan/estaterecords.html
  Brief list for Co. Cavan

- Principal Landed Proprietors 1802
  www.sierratel.com/colinf/genuki/CAV/Proprietors1802.htm
  List for Co. Cavan

Clare

- List of Tenants on Colonel O'Callaghan's Estate, Bodyke, 1890's
  www.clarelibrary.coclare/history/tenants__ocallaghans__estate.htm

Cork

- County Cork: Land and Landholders
  www.sci.net.au/userpages/mgrogan/cork/a__land.htm
  Gateway to a number of local pages

Donegal

- Tenants on the Abercorn Donegal Estate, Laggan Area, Co. Donegal, Ireland, 1794
  freepages.genealogy.rootsweb.com/~donegal/abercorn.htm

Galway

- Estate Records, County Galway
  freepages.genealogy.rootsweb.com/~nyirish/
  Estate%20Records%20County%20Galway.htm
  List of collections

Kerry

- The Kenmare Papers
  proni.nics.gov.uk/records/private/Kenmare.htm
  Estate records of the Kenmare family of Killarney, Co. Kerry; the estate covered much of Co. Kerry, and also various places in Co's. Limerick, Cork, Kilkenny, Laois, Carlow, Tipperary and Clare

Londonderry

- The Drapers Company, Co. Londonderry, Estate Archive
  proni.nics.gov.uk/records/private/drapers.htm

Louth

- County Louth: Tenants of Lord Roden, circa 1837
  www.rootsweb.com/~fianna/county/louth/rodn1837.html

Mayo

- 1815 Town of Westport Rent Roll
  freepages.genealogy.rootsweb.com/~deesegenes/wes.html

- Marquis of Sligo rent roll: Old Head estate, Mayo, 1802
  freepages.genealogy.rootsweb.com/~deesegenes/rent.html

Wexford

- Estate Records, County Wexford
  freepages.genealogy.rootsweb.com/~nyirish/
  Estate%20Records%20County%20Wexford.html
  List of collections

Flax Lists

- Irish Flax Growers List 1796
  www.ancestry.com/search/rectype/inddbs/3732.htm
  Database

Cavan

- 1796 Flax Growers List
  freepages.genealogy.rootsweb.com/~adrian/Cavan/htm
  Scroll down to title. Pages for 48 places in Co. Cavan

Clare

- County Clare: Irish Flax Growers 1796
  www.connorsgenealogy.com/clare/clareflax.htm

Donegal

- The 1796 Spinning Wheel Premium Entitlement List
  freepages.genealogy.rootsweb.com/~donegal/flaxlist1.txt
  For Co. Donegal. See also **/flaxlist2.txt**

Kerry

1796 Flax Seed Premium Entitlement List: County Kerry
www.rootsweb.com/~irlker/flax1796.html

Limerick

- County Limerick: Irish Flax Growers 1796
  www.connorsgenealogy.com/LIM/flaxgrowers.htm

Game Licences

- Game Licences
  www.celticcousins.net/ireland/cl1810g.htm
  List from *Clare journal,* 24 Sept. 1810

- Game Licences: *Freeman's journal,* 27 & 30 September 1809
  members.iinet.net.au/~nickred/lists/Dublin_game_1809.htm
  Issued in Dublin

Grand Jury Records
- Grand Jury Records
  proni.nics.gov.uk/records/grandju.htm
  List for Ulster. The Grand Jury played a major role in local
  government; the records include many lists of names

Griffiths Valuation
- Griffiths Valuation 1848-1864
  members.cox.net/hayes1966/griffiths.htm
  Database; national

- Griffiths Valuation: a 19th century Irish census substitute
  familytreemaker.genealogy.com/30_griff.html?Welcome=991305839
  Description of an important source

- How to Use Griffiths Valuation / Public Record Office of Northern
  Ireland
  proni.nics.gov.uk/research/family/griffith.htm

- The Ireland List Griffiths Valuation Page
  freepages.genealogy.rootsweb.com/~irelandlist/anc.html

- Griffiths Valuation of Ireland Online
  **www.otherdays.com/presentation/archives/
  default.asp?search_a=show&ID=862&current_Cat=0**
  Subscription Database

- The Primary Valuation of Tenements
  freepages.rootsweb.com/~irishancestors/Primary%20Valuation.html

- Valuation Office: Genealogy and Research
  www.valoff.ie/Genealogy.htm
  Brief note on Griffiths Valuation

Antrim
- Ireland Householders Index, County Antrim
  www.ancestry.com/search/db.aspx?dbid=4631
  Index to Griffiths Valuation, and to the tithe applotment books

Carlow
- County Carlow genealogy: Griffiths Evaluations (1852): Union of Carlow
  www.rootsweb.com/~irlcar2/valuations.htm

Clare
- Griffiths Valuation 1855
  www.clarelibrary.ie/eolas/coclare/genealogy/griffiths/griffith.htm
  In Co. Clare

- Index to Griffiths Valuation of Ireland for County Clare
  www.geocities.com/Heartland/Valley/5946/griffith.htm

- Townland Database and Griffiths Valuation
  www.rootsweb.com/~irlcla/villages.html
  For Co. Clare

Cork
- County Cork: Griffiths Valuation of Ireland, 1848-1864
  www.sci.net.au/userpages/mgrogan/cork/a_griffith.htm
  Gateway to pages of transcripts and indexes

- Ginni Swanton's Web Site: Griffiths Valuation
  www.ginnisw.com/griffith4.htm
  For various Co. Cork parishes

- Griffiths Valuation: North West Cork, 1851-1853
  members.cox.net/hayes1966/corknw.htm
  For parishes in N.W. Cork

- Griffiths Evaluation
  www.paulturner.ca/Ireland/Cork/Griffiths/Griffiths.htm
  For Ballymoney and Kinneigh, Co. Cork, 1852

Donegal

- 1857 Griffiths Valuation of Co. Donegal
  freepages.genealogy.rootsweb.com/~donegal/griffiths.htm

- Beagh Parish Griffiths Valuation in 1850's: Heads of Households
  home.att.net/~labaths/griffith.htm

- 1857 Griffith's Valuation: Derrynacarrow East, or Bellanaboy -
  Stranasaggart - Commeen, Donegal, Ireland
  www.geocities.com/Heartland/Estates/6587/Grif1857.html

- Griffiths Valuation for Inishkeeragh, no.359; Cloghcor; Fallagowan;
  Gortgarra
  freepages.genealogy.rootsweb.com/~donegaleire/Dongrifinish.html

- Griffiths Valuation for Templecrone Parish 1857
  freepages.genealogy.rootsweb.com/~donegaleire/Dongrifinish2.html
  Continued in **/Dongrifinish3.html**

Down

- Griffith Valuation: Lawrencetown 1857
  www.lawrencetown.com/griffith.htm

Kerry

- Griffiths Valuations: County Kerry
  www.rootsweb.com/~irlker/griffith.html
  In progress

- Family History Library Film Numbers for (Griffiths) Valuations for
  Kerry County
  www.rootsweb.com/~irlker/griffilm.html

- Notes from Griffiths Valuation for Brusnagh (Brosna), Castleisland,
  Currauns, Killeentierna and Nohavel
  www.rootsweb.com/~irlker

- Griffiths Valuation 1851: Civil Parish of Listowel, Barony of
  Iraghticonnor, County of Kerry
  www.geocities.com/irishancestralpages/gv_listowell_main.html

Leitrim

- Leitrim-Roscommon Griffiths Database
  www.leitrim-roscommon.com/GRIFFITH/

Limerick

- Intro to Griffiths Valuation
  www.geocities.com/jackreidy/grifintr.htm
  For S.W. Co. Limerick

Longford

- Griffiths Valuation (1860+), Union of Ballymahon
  www.rootsweb.com/~irllog/valuations.htm
  Incomplete

Mayo

- Griffiths Valuation for County Mayo
  www.ajmorris.com/dig/toc/mygrif.htm
  Pay per view site

- Griffith Valuation for Co. Mayo
  freepages.genealogy.rootsweb.com/~deesegenes/grif.html
  For a few parishes only

- Online Database: Templemore, Mayo Valuation, 1856-1857
  www.everton.com/FHN/fhn1998/21May98.htm

Roscommon

See Leitrim

Sligo

- Sligo Griffiths Valuation Records
  www.rootsweb.com/~irlsli/griffithsopen.html

- Sligo Griffiths Valuation records
  www.rootsweb.com/~irlsli/index2.html

Tyrone
- Griffiths Valuation Index
  freepages.genealogy.rootsweb.com/~tyrone/parishes/griffiths/
  Covers 8 parishes in Co. Tyrone

Wicklow See also Cork
- Griffiths Valuation April 1854
  www.rootsweb.com/~irlwic/Griff.htm

- Full Name Index to Householders for Griffiths Primary Valuation,
  County Wicklow, Ireland
  www.ajmorris.com/dig/toc/__01wkgi.htm
  Pay per view site

- Griffiths Primary Valuation of Rateable Property for County Wicklow:
  Naas Poor Law Union
  www.ajmorris.com/dig/toc/__01wkns.htm
  Pay per view site

- Griffiths Primary Valuation of Rateable Property for County Wicklow:
  Rathdown Poor Law Union
  www.ajmorris.com/dig/toc/__01wkrd.htm
  Pay per view site

Hearth Tax

Donegal
- A list of persons who paid Hearth Tax in 1665 in the parish of
  Clonleigh, Donegal, Ireland
  freepages.genealogy.rootsweb.com/~donegal/clonleigh.htm

- Householders in Culdaff who paid a Hearth Tax in 1665
  freepages.genealogy.rootsweb.com/~donegal/culdaffhearth.htm

- The Hearth Money Roll for the Parish of Donoughmore, Donegal ... in
  1665
  freepages.genealogy.rootsweb.com/~donegal/hdonough.htm
  thor.prohosting.com/~hughw/donoughm.txt

- Hearth Money Roll, 1665 for the parish of Leck, in the Barony of
  Raphoe, Co. Donegal, Ireland
  thor.prohosting.com/~hughw/leck1665.txt

- Hearth Money Roll 1665 for the parish of Leck in the Barony of
  Raphoe, Co. Donegal
  freepages.genealogy.rootsweb.com/~donegal/leck1665.htm

- 1665 Hearth Money Roll for Lettermacaward
  freepages.genealogy.rootsweb.com/~donegal/letterhr.htm

- Persons who paid Hearth Tax in the parish of Raphoe (including)
  Convoy, in Co. Donegal, Ireland in the year 1665
  freepages.genealogy.rootsweb.com/~donegal/raphoe.htm
  thor.prohosting.com/~hughw/raphoe.txt

- 1665 hearth money roll for Templecrone
  freepages.genealogy.rootsweb.com/~donegal/templehr.htm

- Persons who paid Hearth Money Tax in the parish of Taughboyne,
  Barony of Raphoe, Co. Donegal, Ireland, in 1665
  freepages.genealogy.rootsweb.com/taughboy.htm
  thor.prohosting.com/~hughw/taughboy.txt

Tipperary
- 1664 Hearth Money Rolls for the Baronies of Ida and Offa, Co.
  Tipperary
  freepages.genealogy.rootsweb.com/~irish/Tipperary/1664iffa.htm

Tyrone

- Hearth Money: Dungannon
freepages.genealogy.rootsweb.com/~tyrone/info/
hearth-money-dungannon.html

Land Records

- Land Records
scripts.ireland.com/ancestor/browse/records/land

- Names of the Cromwellian Adventurers for land in Ireland
www.exis.net/ahd/monaghan/advntrs.htm
In 1642-6; list of surnames

- Lands Grants in the Barony of Raphoe, County Donegal, 1608
members.aol.com/dngl1608.html

- Pynnar's Survey, 1618 A.D. of the land grants given in 1608, Barony of Raphoe
members.aol.com/Manus/dng1618.html

Landowners Census

- Land Owners in Ireland
www.ajmorris.com/dig/toc/__01irlo.htm
Pay per view site. Scanned images of the entire 1876 landowners census

Armagh

- Landowners in Co. Armagh circa 1870's
www.rootsweb.com/~nirarm/landowners.html

Cavan

- 1876 Land Owners
www.sierratel.com/colinf/genuki/CAV/1876Land.html

Clare

- Land Owners in Clare: return of owners of land of one acre and upwards in County Clare, 1876
www.clarelibrary.ie/eolas/coclare/genealogy/
land__owners__in__clare.htm

Cork

- Land Owners in Ireland 1876: County Cork
www.ginnisw.com/Cork%20Landowners%201876/Thumb/Thumbs1.htm
Facsimile of the Parliamentary paper

- Return of Owners of Land ... 1876: Mallow
www.rootsweb.com/~irlmahs/mloii.htm

Donegal

- 1876 Landowners Donegal
www.ulsterancestry.com/1876__Landowners__Co-Donegal.html

Galway

- Landowners in Co. Galway, circa 1870's
www.rootsweb.com/~irlgal/Landowners.html

Longford

- Landowners of County Longford in the 1870's
www.rootsweb.com/~irllog/landown.htm

Roscommon

- Landowners of Roscommon County in 1871
www.rootsweb.com/~irlros/returnof.htm

Sligo

- Land Owners in Co. Sligo, late 1870's
www.rootsweb.com/~irlsli/landowners.html

Tipperary

- Property Owners County Tipperary since 1870
www.cmcrp.net/Tipperary/Landowner1.html

Waterford

- Landowners of Waterford (1876)
www.rootsweb.com/~irlwat2/landowners.htm

Westmeath

- Landowners in Co. Westmeath, circa 1870's
www.rootsweb.com/~irlwem/Landowners.html

Wicklow

- Clever Cat Genealogy Data
  www.rootsweb.com/~irlwic2/
  Click on 'landowners in Wicklow 1876'. Primarily the landowners
  return of 1876

Loyalist Claims

- Claims of 1798 Loyalists
  www.geocities.com/Heartland/Park/7461/claim1798.html
  In Burrishoole, Co. Mayo

Marriage Licence Bonds

Cavan

- Church of Ireland. Marriage Licence Bonds. Diocese of Kilmore &
  Ardagh
  freepages.genealogy.rootsweb.com/~adrian/ColKilm.htm
  For 1697-1844

Clare

- Killaloe, Co. Clare Marriage License Bonds, 1680-1720 and 1760-1762
  home.att.net/~labaths/killaloe.htm

Dublin

- Church of Ireland Marriage Licenses from Diocese of Dublin 1638-1794
  www.rootsweb.com/~irllex/groom.htm

- Dublin Prerogative Marriage Licences (also called marriage bonds)
  www.rootsweb.com/~irllex/dublin__bonds.htm

Fermanagh

See Tyrone

Laois

- Church of Ireland Marriage Licences from Diocese of Dublin, 1638-1764
  www.rootsweb.com/~irllex/groom.htm
  For Co.Laois

- Laois Marriage Bonds from the Dioceses of Ferns, Ossory & Leighlin,
  A-D
  www.rootsweb.com/~irllex/ossory__bonds.htm

Longford

- Church of Ireland Marriage Licences from Diocese of Dublin, 1732-1757
  www.rootsweb.com/~irllog/groom.htm
  For Co. Longford

Meath

- Church of Ireland. Marriage Licence Bonds. Diocese of Meath
  freepages.genealogy.rootsweb.com/~adrian/ColMeath.htm
  For 1665-1844

Tipperary

- Church of Ireland Marriage Licences from Diocese of Dublin
  (Tipperary names) 1638-1794
  www.rootsweb.com/~irltip2/groom.htm

- Diocese of Killaloe Marriage Licence Bonds 1680-1762 (Tipperary
  names)
  www.rootsweb.com/~irltip2/killaloe.htm

Tyrone

- Church of Ireland Marriage Licence Bonds. Diocese of Clogher
  freepages.genealogy.rootsweb.com/~adrian/ColClog.htm
  For 1709-1866

- Church of Ireland Marriage Licence Bonds: Diocese of Clogher Extracts
  www.ulsterancestry.com/
  Church__of__Ireland__Marriage__Licence__Bonds.html
  Covers Cos. Tyrone and Fermanagh, and parts of Armagh, Cavan &
  Monaghan, 18-19th c.

Ulster

- Church of Ireland Marriage Licence Bonds: Diocese of Kilmore & Ardagh
  www.ulsterancestry.com/ua-free__MarriageLicenceBonds.html
  Covers parts of Cos. Armagh, Cavan, Leitrim, Monaghan, Sligo, *etc.* 18-19th c.

Westmeath

- Church of Ireland Marriage Licences from Diocese of Dublin, 1680-1764
  www.rootsweb.com/~irlwem2/groom.htm
  From Westmeath

Methodist Records

- The Donegall Square Methodist Church Papers
  proni.nics.gov.uk/records/private/method.htm

Muster Rolls

Cavan

- 1630 Muster Roll, Co. Cavan
  freepages.genealogy.rootsweb.com/~adrian/Must1630.htm

Donegal

- The Muster Roll of the County of Donnagall 1630 A.D., as printed in the *Donegal Annual*
  www.ulsterancestry.com/MusterRoll-1630.html

Fermanagh

- Muster Rolls of Co. Fermanagh
  www.rootsweb.com/~nirfer2/military__1630.htm

- From the Muster Roll of the County of Fermanagh 1631
  www.ulsterancestry.com/muster-roll__1663.html

Londonderry

- County Derry 1631 Muster Roll
  www.rootsweb.com/~fianna/county/derry/ldy-1631.html

- Muster Roll on the Ironmongers Estate, Co. Londonderry, Ireland, (circa 1630)
  www.rootsweb.com/~nirldy/aghadowey/ironmust.htm

Newspapers

- Newspapers
  scripts.ireland.com/ancestor/browse/records/news/

- Newspapers
  www.iol.ie/dublincitylibrary/ganewspapers.htm
  In Dublin City Library

- A Guide to Newspapers in PRONI
  proni.nics.gov.uk/records/newspaper.htm

- Newspaper Abstracts: Ireland
  www.newspaperabstracts.com/ireland/
  Mainly 19th c.

- Norman Ross Publishing Inc. Irish Newspapers on 35 mm. silver holide positive film from the British Library's Newspaper Library Colindale
  www.nross.com/newsiri1.htm
  Historic Irish newspapers available for purchase

- The *Belfast Newsletter* index 1737-1800
  www.ucs.louisiana.edu/bnl

- Newspapers
  home.pacbell.net/nymets11/genuki/CLA/Newspapers.html
  List for Co. Clare

- Index to Biographical Notices in the *Clare Champion* newspaper 1935-1985
  www.clarelibrary.ie/eolas/coclare/genealogy/champions/champion.htm

- Limerick Chronicle Obituaries 1850
  uk.geocities.com/irishancestralpages/lc1850main.html

- The Newspaper Collection
  ireland.iol.ie/%Etipplibs/Newspapr.htm
  Of Tipperary Libraries

Petitions
- 1916 Petition to split Knocknagoshel from the Diocese of Brosna
  www.rootsweb.com/~irlker/parishpet.html

- [Clare Men in Favour of Union of Britain and Ireland 1799]
  www.celticcousins.net/ireland/1799cl.htm
  List from the *Ennis Chronicle*

Photographs
- Photographic Records
  proni.nics.gov.uk/records/photo.htm

Plantation Records
- Plantation of County Cavan
  www.sierratel.com/colinf/genuki/CAV/Plantation.html
  List of grantees of lands, 1612-13

Plea Rolls
- The Medieval Irish Plea Rolls: an introduction
  www.nationalarchives.ie/pleas__1.html

Poll Tax
- County Donegal Surname on the Census, 1659: Poll Money Ordinances
  www.geocities.com/Heartland/Estates/6587/Doncensus.html

Poor Law
- An Introduction to the Poor Law and its Records
  www.local.ie/content/52105.shtml/genealogy/
  irish__records/census__substitutes

- The Workhouse in Ireland
  users.ox.ac.uk/~peter/workhouse/ireland.html
  Includes page for each union, listing records (click on 'union lists' at bottom of page)

- Workhouses
  www.rootsweb.com/~fianna/guide/PLUwork.html
  List of Irish records

- Poor Law Records
  proni.nics.gov.uk/records/poor__law.htm
  In the Public Record Office of Northern Ireland

Presbyterian Records
- Index to Presbyterian Church Records
  proni.nics.gov.uk/records/private/presindx.htm
  Parish records held by the Public Record Office of Northern Ireland

Roman Catholic Records
- Local Catholic Church and Family History - Genealogy Ireland
  home.att.net/~Local__Catholic/Catholic-Ireland.htm
  Includes list of counties with their dioceses, much historical information, and many links

School Records and Registers
- National School Records
  www.nationalarchives.ie/Nat__Schools/natschs.html
  Details of records in the National Archives

- 1824 Survey of Irish Schools
  www.rootsweb.com/~irlker/schoolsur.html
  General discussion of a source for teachers

Donegal
- Register of the old Killybegs Commons School
  freepages.genealogy.rootsweb.com/~donegal/killybegsns.htm

- Raphoe Royal School: students names
  freepages.genealogy.rootsweb.com/~donegaleire/Rapschool.html
  In 1849

Down
- The Old School Registers: Lawrencetown Male National School,
  1870 to 1898
  www.lawrencetown.com/reg1.htm

- The Old School Registers: Lawrencetown Female National School,
  1880 to 1923
  www.lawrencetown.com/reg2.htm

Limerick
- Sacred Heart College 1859-1909
  home.att.net/
         ~JMcCarthy/sacred__heart__college__limerick.htm#pupils1859
  List of pupils of a Limerick School

- Schools and School Teachers: Murroe and Boher, Co. Limerick, 1852-1964
  www.geocities.com/irishancestralpages/murbohlim.html

Meath
- Ashbourne National School Register of Names from 1870 to 1906
  www.angelfire.com/ak2/ashbourne/reginfs1.html

Tyrone
- Schools Index
  freepages.genealogy.rootsweb.com/~tyrone/schools/
  Miscellaneous sources relating to schools in Co. Tyrone

Ulster
- School Records
  proni.nics.gov.uk/records/school.htm
  In Ulster

Solicitors Records
- Solicitors Records
  proni.nics.gov.uk/records/solicit.htm
  In the Public Record Office of Northern Ireland

- The O'Rorke, McDonald & Tweed Archive
  proni.nics.gov.uk/records/private/d-1242.htm
  Solicitors archives relative to Co. Antrim

- The Martin & Brett Archive
  proni.nics.gov.uk/records/private/marbrett.htm
  Description of a solicitor's archive relating to Co. Monaghan

Tithes
- Tithe Composition and Applotment Books
  freepages.genealogy.rootsweb.com/~irishancestors/Tithe%20books.html
  Introduction

- Tithe Applotment Books and Primary Valuation
  www.nationalarchives.ie/titheapplprimvalu.html
  From the National Archives

- The Tithe Defaulters, 1831
  www.ancestordetective.com/ireland/tithe.htm
  Discussion of a useful source.

- Ireland: a listing of Land Tax or Tithe Defaulters for 1831
  www.alphalink.com.au/~datatree/datree1.htm
  Description of the source; not the names themselves

- Tithe Applotment Records
  proni.nics.gov.uk/records/tithe.htm
  For Ulster

Carlow
- County Carlow Tithe Defaulters for 1831
  www.rootsweb.com/~irlcar2/Tithe__Defaulters.htm

Cork
- County Cork Tithes
  www.sci.net.au/userpages/mgrogan/cork/a__tithes.htm
  Many pages of transcripts of tithe applotment books for particular places

- Ginni Swanton's Web Site: Tithe Applotment Records, parish of Desertserges, Diocese of Cork April 1829
  www.ginnisw.com/tithe.htm

- 1827 Tithe Applotment Book for the Parish of Inchigeelagh (Iveleary) County Cork
  www.sci.net.au/userpages/mgrogan/cork/inchigeelagh.htm

Donegal
- Tithe Applotment Books for the Parishes of Killybegs, Upper and Lower
  freepages.genealogy.rootsweb.com/~donegal/killytithe.txt

- Tithe Applotment Book for the Parish of Templecrone, signed 22 Oct. 1828
  freepages.genealogy.rootsweb.com/~donegal/templetithes.txt

- Templecrone Parish Records for Tithe and Griffiths Valuation
  www.odonnell-world.com/genealogy/mayo-templecrone-tithe-list.htm

Kerry
- Tithe Applotment Survey 1823-37: County Kerry
  www.rootsweb.com/~irlker/tithe.html
  In progress

- Heads of Household of Ballyferriter Catholic Parish, Barony of Corkaguiny, County Kerry, Ireland, 1827-1852
  www.geocities.com/Athens/Ithaca/7974/Ballyferriter/compilation.htm
  From tithe applotment books 1827-31, a religious census 1834, and Griffiths Valuation 1851-2.

- Tithe Valuation, Brosna Parish, Co. Kerry, Ireland, c.1820
  www.geocities.com/bluegumtrees/griffiths.html

Limerick
- Tithe Records, 1820's: Killeedy, Co. Limerick
  www.geocities.com/curtingenealogy/titheKilleedy.html

Sligo
- Sligo Tithe Applotment Book
  www.rootsweb.com/~irlsli/index2.html

- Tithe Applotment Book: Parish of Easky
  www.rootsweb.com/~irlsli/tithe1.html
  Continued in **/tithe2.html/c.1833**

Tipperary
- The Parish of Outeragh, County Tipperary, Ireland
  www.ancestordetective.com/ireland/outeragh.htm
  Based on Tithe Applotment Book, Griffiths Valuation, etc.

Tyrone
- Tithe Applotment Explanation
  freepages.genealogy.rootsweb.com/~tyrone/parishes/tithe-applotment/
  List of applotments for Co. Tyrone, including some transcripts

Transportation Records
- Transportation Records 1791-1853
  freepage.genealogy.rootsweb.com/~irishancestors/AusT.html

- Australian Transport Records: National Library of Ireland 1791-1853
  www.ajmorris.com/dig/web/autp.htm
  For subscribers only

- National Archives of Ireland Transportation Records Database
  www.nationalarchives.ie/search01.html
  Transportation to Australia

- Sources in the National Archives for Research into the Transportation of Irish Convicts to Australia (1791-1853)
  www.nationalarchives.ie/transp1.html
  Research guide from the National Archive of Ireland

- Irish Rebels to Australia 1797-1806
  www.pcug.org.au/~ppmay/rebels.htm
  Database

- Irish Convicts to N.S.W. 1791-1825
  www.pcug.org.au/~ppmay/convicts.htm

- Larry Brennan's Page
  www.rootsweb.com/~irlcla/ClareConvictsToAustralia.html
  Co. Clare convicts transported to Australia

- Genseek: Ratcliffe Convicts 1845
  www.standard.net.au/~jwilliams/rat.htm
  List of Irish convicts who arrived in Tasmania in 1845

Donegal
- National Archives of Ireland: Convicts from Donegal to Australia covering the period 1788 to 1868
  freepages.genealogy.rootsweb.com/~donegal/iconoz.txt
  List

- People Involuntarily Transported to America from Donegal 1737 to 1743
  freepages.genealogy.rootsweb.com/~donegal/involtrans.htm

Louth
- County Louth. Dundalk Householders 1837
  www.rootsweb.com/~fianna/county/louth/loufree1837.html
  From Valuation Office House Book

Roscommon
- Criminals Transported to Australia, 1836 to 1853
  www.rootsweb.com/~irlros/transported.htm
  From Co. Roscommon

Ulster Covenant
- The Ulster Covenant
  www.proni.gov.uk/ulstercovenant/
  Database of c.500,000 signatures to the 1912 Ulster Covenant

Valuation Records
- Valuation Records
  proni.nics.gov.uk/records/valuatn.htm
  Details of various land valuation records in the Public Record Offices of Northern Ireland 19-20th c.

Wills
- Probate in Ireland, Part 1: from 1858
  www.ancestry.com/library/view/news/articles/2515.asp

- Probate in Ireland, part 2: Up to 1857
  www.ancestry.com/library/view/news/articles/2923.asp

- Wills
  scripts.ireland.com/ancestor/browse/records/wills
  General introduction

- Wills and Administrations
  www.nationalarchives.ie/willsandadmin.html
  From the National Archives

- Index to the Prerogative Wills of Ireland 1536-1810
  www.ajmorris.com/dig/toc/__01iwpr.htm
  Pay per view site. From a published source

- Wills and Testamentary Records
  proni.nics.gov.uk/records/wills.htm
  Wills in the Public Record Office of Northern Ireland

Cavan
- County Cavan: Probate
  www.sierratel.com/colinf/genuki/CAV/Probate.html
  Where to look

List by Diocese
- Wills in the Diocese of Ardfert and Aghadoe
  www.ajmorris.com/dig/toc/__01iw3e.htm
  Pay per view site. Index from published source

- Wills in the Diocese of Cashel and Emly
  www.ajmorris.com/dig/toc/__01iw3a.htm
  Pay per view site. Index from a published source

- Wills in the Diocese of Clonfert
  www.ajmorris.com/dig/toc/__01iwcl.htm
  Pay per view site. Index from a published source

- Wills in the Diocese of Cloyne
  www.ajmorris.com/dig/toc/__01iw2b.htm
  Pay per view site. Index from a published source

- Wills in the Diocese of Cork and Ross
  www.ajmorris.com/dig/toc/__01iw2a.htm
  Pay per view site. Index from a published source

- *Indexes to Irish wills, volume II: Cork and Ross, Cloyne,* ed.
  W.P.W. Phillimore
  www.ginnisw.com/
  Click on 'index to Irish wills'. Facsimile; published Phillimore & Co.,
  1910

- Wills in the Diocese of Derry
  www.ajmorris.com/dig/toc/__01iw5a.htm
  Pay per view site. Index from a published source

- Wills in the Diocese of Dromore
  www.ajmorris.com/dig/toc/__01iw4a.htm
  Pay per view site. Index from a published source

- Wills and Marriage Licences, Dublin Diocese 1270-1857
  www.otherdays.com/presentation/archive/
  default.asp?search__a=show&id=1309

- Wills in the Diocese of Ferns
  www.ajmorris.com/dig/toc/__01iw1c.htm
  Pay per view site. Index from a published source

- Wills in the Diocese of Kildare
  www.ajmorris.com/dig/toc/__01iw1d.htm
  Pay per view site. Index from a published source

- Killala and Achonry Diocese Wills, County Sligo
  www.rootsweb.com/%7Eirlsli/willssligohome.html
  List

- Wills in the Diocese of Killaloe and Kilfernara
  www.ajmorris.com/dig/toc/__01iw3c.htm
  Pay per view site. Index from a published source

- Wills in the Diocese of Leighlin
  www.ajmorris.com/dig/toc/__01iw1b.htm
  Pay per view site. Index from a published source

- Wills in the Diocese of Limerick
  www.ajmorris.com/dig/toc/__01iw3d.htm
  Pay per view site. Index from a published source

- Wills in the Diocese of Ossory
  www.ajmorris.com/dig/toc/__01iw1a.htm
  Pay per view site. Index from a published source

- Wills in the Diocese of Raphoe
  www.ajmorris.com/dig/toc/__01iw5b.htm
  Pay per view site. Wills from a published source

- Index of Wills, Diocese of Raphoe 1684-1858
  freepages.genealogy.rootsweb.com/~donegal/wills.htm

- Donegal Will Index: Diocese of Raphoe, 1684-1858
  www.ulsterancestry.com/ua-free-Donegal/WillIndex.html

- Wills in the Diocese of Waterford and Lismore
  www.ajmorris.com/dig/toc/__01iw3b.htm
  Pay per view site. Index from a published source

12. Occupational Records

The occupations of our ancestors generated an immense amount of documentation, much of which is of value to the family historian. An introduction to these sources is provided by:

- Occupational Records
  scripts.ireland.com/ancestor/browse/records/occupation

Clergy
Donegal
- Clergy of Templecrune, Arranmore, Falcarragh, Killult, Raymunterdoney and Tullaghobegley to 1900
  freepages.genealogy.rootsweb.com/~donegal/clergy.htm

Kerry
- List of 'Popish Parish Priests' in Kerry, 1704
  www.rootsweb.com/~irlker/popish.html

Convicts & Prisoners
- Out of the Jails: Irishmen Again Free
  home.att.net/~J-McCarthy/1922__out__of__the__jails.htm
  List of Irish prisoners released in 1922

- Trials, Convicts, Transportees, Co.Clare, 1842-1850
  www.otherdays.com/presentation/asp/search/
  presAffOther.asp?dbid=178

  Pay per view database

- 1849 Mayo Convictions
  freepages.genealogy.rootsweb.com/~deesegenes/convict.html
  List of convicts

- Genseek Return of Prisoners found Guilty at Spring Assizes 1845, Neenagh, Co. Tipperary
  www.standard.net.au/~jwilliams/pris45.htm

- Neenagh Gaol: Removal of Convicts
  www.standard.net.au/~jwilliams/tgaol.htm
  List, 1845

- Wicklow United Irishmen 1797-1804
  www.pcug.org.au/~ppmay/wicklow.htm
  Database of convicts

Freeholders
- Freeholders Records
  www.proni.gov.uk/freeholders/intro.asp
  Discussion of a source which lists those entitled to vote, or who did vote

- Freeholders in the Queens County from 1 Jan. 1758-1 Dec. 1775
  www.rootsweb.com/~irllex/freeholders.htm

- County Louth Freeholders 1822
  www.rootsweb.com/~fianna/county/louth/loufree1822.html

- County Louth Freeholders 1824 (supplementary records)
  www.rootsweb.com/~fianna/county/louth/loufree1824.html

- List of Freeholders of the County of Tipperary in the year 1776
  www.rootsweb.com/irltip2/freeholders.htm

Landowners
- Landowners Map of County Kilkenny, c.1640
  www.rootsweb.com/~irlkik/landomap.htm

Medical Practitioners
- The Medical Directory for Ireland 1858
  www.nationalarchivist.com
  Forthcoming. Click on 'Directories and Professionals' and title

Militia & Yeomanry
- Militia, Yeomanry Lists, and Muster Rolls
  proni.nics.gov.uk/records/militia.htm
  List of sources for Ulster

- Cavan Militia
  www.sierratel.com/colinf/genuki/CAV/Military/Militia.html
  Notes on genealogical sources; includes brief list of Chelsea Pensioners

Patients
- Simpsons Hospital Applications 1817-1847
  www.otherdays.com/presentation/asp/search/presAffOther.asp?dbid=121
  Pay per view database of patients admitted to a Dublin hospital

- Simpsons Hospital Departuress 1817-1933
  www.otherdays.com/presentation/asp/search/presAffOther.asp?dbid=123

Pawnbrokers
- Pawnbrokers in Limerick 1837 & 1877
  home.att.net/~tcdman/limerick__pawnbrokers.htm

Police
- Royal Irish Constabulary Records
  catalogue.pro.gov.uk/leaflets/ri2161.htm

- Royal Irish Constabulary (Directories) 1824-1910
  www.otherdays.com/presentation/asp/search/presAffOther.asp?dbid=203
  Pay per view database

- Royal Irish Constabulary officers 1849
  www.otherdays.com/presentation/archive/default.asp?search__a=show&id=1438
  Pay per view database

- Police History.com
  www.esatclear.ie/~garda/
  www.geocities.com/CapitolHill/7900/

- Police Service of Northern Ireland: Police Museum
  www.psni.police.uk/index/pg__police__museum.htm
  Includes page on service records, 1822-1922. Click on 'genealogy
  information'

- Royal Irish Constabulary: Cork Appointees 1816-1840
  www.sci.net.au/userpages/mgrogan/cork/ric__vol1.htm
  Continued at **/ric__vol2.htm**
  and **/ric__vol3.htm**

Kerry
- Kerry R.I.C. Record Excerpts for 1848-1852
  www.rootsweb.com/~irlker/ric.html
  Co. Kerry police

Longford
- Award of Pensions
  www.rootsweb.com/~irllog/police.htm
  On disbandment of the Royal Irish Constabulary in Co.Longford, 1919

Postmen
- Postmasters and Post Offices, Ireland, 1849
  www.otherdays.com/presentation/asp/search/
  presAffOther.asp?dbid=221

  Pay per view database

Publicans
- Publicans, Brewers, Distillers, 1823-1910 (South)
  www.otherdays.com/presentation/asp/search/
  presAffOther.asp?dbid=200

  Pay per view database

Revenue Commissioners
- Irish Revenue Commissioners 1709
  www.from-ireland.net/lists/revenue%20officers%20ireland%201709.htm

Soldiers
- Finding and Using Irish Military Records
  www.rootsweb.com/~fianna/guide/military.html

- Register and Index of Irish Regiments
  www.regiments.org/milhist/regtintro/rgtirish.htm

- Irish Cavalry Regiments
  www.sci.net.au/userpages/mgrogan/cork/regiment.htm
  List of regiments with brief notes

- King James's Irish Army List
  www.irishroots.com/id4233.htm

- Genealogy Quest, Ireland: Roman Catholic Officers 1693
  www.genealogy-quest.com/collections/rcoffi.html

- The Irish Pensioners of William III's Huguenot Regiments, 1702
  home.att.net/~cmlabath/huguenotpensioners.htm

- Civil War Rosters: Irish Regiments
  www.geocities.com/Area51/Lair/3680/cw/irish.html
  Names of soldiers in the U.S. Civil War

- 1832 Military Index, Ireland
  www.from-ireland.net/history/allcounties/1832military.htm

- North Clare Soldiers in Word War I
  www.clarelibrary.ie/colas/coclare/history/soldiers/
  north__clare__soldiers.htm

- Cork Battalion 1916
  freepages.genealogy.rootsweb.com/~bwickham/corkbatt.htm

- WWI Officers from Co. Kerry
  www.rootsweb.com/~irlker/ww1officer.html

- World War I Wexford Casualties
  freepages.genealogy.rootsweb.com/~nyirish/Wexford%20Casualties%20WWI.html

- Irish Officers in the United States Army, 1865-1898
  www.rootsweb.com/~irlker/officers1865.html

- The Irish in Korea: Irish men and women who gave their lives in the Korean War
  www.illyria.com/irishkos.html

Surgeons
- Brief Summary of the Resources at the Royal College of Surgeons
  www.rootsweb.com/~irldubli/RoyalCollege.htm

Teachers
- Teachers and Schools 1823-1910 (Southern Ireland)
  www.otherdays.com/presentation/asp/search/presAffOther.asp?dbid=199

  Pay per view database

Vietnam Veterans
- The Irish on the Wall: Irish men and women whose names are on the Vietnam Veterans Memorial (the Wall) in Washington, D.C.
  www.irishonthewall.com

13. Miscellaneous Sites

Administrative Areas
- Administrative Areas of the British Isles
  www.genuki.org.uk/big/Regions
  Includes pages on the Republic of Ireland, and Northern Ireland

- Administrative Divisions in Ireland
  www.ancestry.com/library/view/news/articles/2435.asp

- The Ire Atlas Townland Database
  www.seanruad.com
  Database of townlands, parishes, counties, baronies, etc.

- O.S. Parish List
  www.nationalarchives.ie/cgi-bin/naigenform02?index=OS+Parish+List

- Geographical Index Northern Ireland
  proni.nics.gov.uk/geogindx.htm
  Locates townlands, parishes, baronies & Poor Law Unions, *etc.*

- The Townland
  proni.nics.gov.uk/research/local/townland.htm
  Discussion of an important local administrative area

- Clare Parishes
  www.clarelibrary.ie/colas/coclare/places/parishes.htm
  Gazetteer of civil parishes

- Townlands of Donegal, listed by Parish
  www.geocities.com/Heartland/Estates/6587/Dontown.html
  List

- Limerick Land Divisions
  home.pacbell.net/nymets11/genuki/LIM/land/landdivisions.htm
  Details of local government areas - townlands, baronies, civil parishes, and poor law unions

- Tir Eoghain/Tyrone
  members.aol.com/lawlerc/tyrone-parishes.html
  List of civil, Roman Catholic, Church of Ireland, and Presbyterian
  parishes, townships, baronies and unions

Adoption
- Irish Adoption Contact Register
  www.adoptionireland.com

- Searching in Ireland
  www.netreach.net/~steed/search.html
  For Irish-born adoptees

Anglo-Irish
- Anglo-Irish Families in Kilkenny County (1300)
  www.rootsweb.com/__irlkik/kfamily.htm

Biographical Information
- Prominent Persons Index
  proni.nics.gov.uk/records/private/ppi.htm
  Information on 5,000 people

Casey Collection
- Casey Collection extracts
  www.rootsweb.com/~irlker/caseyrec.html
  For Co. Kerry

- Kerry Records in the Casey Collection
  www.rootsweb.com/~irlker/casey.html

Chapman Codes
- Chapman Codes for Ireland
  www.genuki.org.uk/big/irl/codes.html

Easter Rising
- Ireland: the Easter Rising 1916
  catalogue.pro.gov.uk/leaflets/ri2065.htm

Famine
- The Great Famine 1845-50. Introduction
  www.nationalarchives.ie/famine.html

Gazetteers
- Ireland Gazetteer and Surname Guide
  www.ancestry.com/search/rectype/inddbs/3856.htm

Heraldry
- Coats of Arms in Ireland and around the world
  homepage.tinet.ie/~donnaweb

- Irish Genealogy & Coats of Arms
  www.ireland-information.com/heraldichall/irishcoatsofarms.htm

- Office of the Chief Herald
  www.nli.ie/fr__offi.htm

- Proto-Heraldry in Early Christian Ireland: the Battle Standards of
  Gaelic Irich Chieftains
  www2.smumn.edu/uasal.IRHERALD.html

Clare
- Heraldry and Families of County Clare
  www.clarelibrary.ie/eolas/coclare/genealogy/herald.htm

Homicides
- Homicides from 1848-1870 in County Westmeath
  www.rootsweb.com/~irlwem2/wstmurd.html

Huguenots
- French Huguenot Sources
  freepages.genealogy.rootsweb.com/≈irishancestors/Hug.html
  Brief introduction

- The Huguenot Society of Great Britain and Ireland
  www.local.ie/content/27567.shtml

- Huguenot Surnames
  www.rootsweb.com/~fianna/surname/hug1.html

- 1696-1996. St. Paul's Church, Arlington. The French Church
  ireland.iol.ie/~offaly/stpauls.htm

Jews
- The Jews of Ireland Genealogy Page
  homepage.tinet.ie/~researchers

Journals and Newsletters
- Irish Journals with Genealogical Content
  www.from-ireland.net/journalcontent.htm
  Valuable listing

- Archaeological and Historical Journals
  www.xs4all.nl/~tbreen/journals.html
  Many of the journals mentioned here have genealogical content

- Irish Chronicles Project
  www.ajmorris.com/dig/toc/__011icp.htm
  Email journal, with many transcripts and indexes of original sources.
  Pay per view site

- The Irish Link: Family History Magazine
  www.netspace.net.au/~gwenoc/

- All Ireland Sources Newsletter
  www.sag.org.au/new/aisn.htm
  Email newsletter published by the Society of Australian Genealogists

- Irish Roots Magazine Homepage
  www.irishrootsmagazine.com
  Includes contents listing

- Local Ancestors Newsletter
  www.local.ie/general/genealogy/local__ancestors/index.shtml
  Email newsletter

- O'Lochlainns Irish Family Journal
  www.irishroots.com

- The Cavan Genealogist
  ireland.iol.ie/~kevins/geneo/index__geneo.html
  Email newsletter

Knights
- Knights Bachelor knighted in Ireland
  www.rootsweb.com/~fianna/surname/knights.html

Local History
- Local and Parish Histories of Ireland
  www.irishgenealogy.com/ireland/parish-histories.htm

- Island Ireland directory for Irish Local History
  islandireland.com/Pages/history/local.html
  Gateway to Irish local history

Look-Ups
- Books We Own: Ireland & Northern Ireland
  www.rootsweb.com/~bwo/ireland.html

Carlow
- County Carlow Lookups
  www.rootsweb.com/~irlcar2/lookup.htm

Clare
- County Clare, County Limerick Lookup Service
  www.connorsgenealogy.com/lookups.html
  Lookups offered on various databases

Galway
- Galway County Look-up Page
  www.rootsweb.com/~irlgal/index1.html

Kerry
- County Kerry Lookups
  www.rootsweb.com/~irlker/lookup.html

Kilkenny
- County Kilkenny Lookup Service
  www.rootsweb.com/~irlkik/klookup.htm

Limerick
See Clare

Mayo
- Mayo County Lookups
  www.geocities.com/Heartland/Acres/4031/Lookups.html

Sligo
- County Sligo: Ireland: Lookups by Volunteers
  www.rootsweb.com/%7Eirlsli/lookup.html

Tipperary
- County Tipperary Lookups
  www.rootsweb.com/~irltip2/

Maps
- Maps of the Counties of Ireland from *A Topographical Dictionary of Ireland,* by Samuel Lewis 1837
  indigo.ie/~rcd/lewismaps.html

- [Maps of Ireland from *Cassells gazetteer* 1899]
  indigo.ie/~rcd/cassells.htm

- Ordnance Survey Ireland
  www.irlgov.ie/osi

- Archives of the Ordnance Survey: List of Parishes and Reference Numbers
  www.nationalarchives.ie/cgi-bin/naigenform02?index=OS+Parish+Lists

- Tom's Big Chest of Old Irish Maps
  homepage.ntlworld.com/tomals/Irish__maps__of__S__Lewis__1839.htm
  Samuel Lewis's county maps, c.1839

Pedigrees
- Irish Pedigrees
  www.ajmorris.com/dig/toc/__01ip00.htm
  Pay per view site. Scanned pages from the book by John O'Hart

- Burke's Irish Family Records
  www.fermanagh.org.uk/genealogy/resources/burkeifr.htm
  Lists 514 family histories in the book

- Milesian Genealogies
  www.rootsweb.com/~fianna/history/milesian.html
  Medieval pedigrees

Peerage & Nobility
- Peerages in Ireland during the 17th Century
  www.rootsweb.com/~fianna/surname/dhpeerages.html

- Uasal: a source for Irish Nobility, Heraldry and Genealogy
  www2.smumn.edu/uasal/noble.html

Scots-Irish
- Our Scotch-Irish Heritage
  members.aol.com/ntgen/hrtg/scirish.html

- The Scots/Irish immigration of the 1700's
  www.zekes.com/%7Edspidell/famresearch/ulster.html
  Discussion

- Scotch-Irish Research
  www.genealogy.com/00000384.html?Welcome=991306619
  Presbyterian Scots in Ulster

Settlers
- Some of the Earliest Settlers in the Laggan Area of Co. Donegal, Ireland
  thor.prohosting.com/~hughw/laggan.txt

Surnames

- Ancient Irish Surnames
  www.rootsweb.com/~fianna/surname/old.html

- An Atlas of Irish Names
  www.ucc.ie/research/atlas/INDEX.HTM
  Study of the origins and distribution of surnames

- Common Names in Ireland during the 17th century
  www.rootsweb.com/~fianna/surname/dhnames2.html

- Hylit Irish Names
  www.hylit.com/info/Names
  Meanings of forenames

- Irish Family Surnames
  www.ulsterancestry.com/irish-names/
  Derivations of common surnames

- Irish Name Locator: 11th to 16th centuries
  www.rootsweb.com/%7Efianna/surname/nam01.html

- Irish Names: traditional, modern, and in-between
  www.namenerds.com/irish/
  Meanings of first names

- Irish Surname Pages
  www.geocities.com/Athens/Parthenon/6108/surnames.htm
  Gateway to sites on specific surnames

- Irish Surnames
  freepages.genealogy.rootsweb.com/≈irishancestors/Surnames/

- Norman and Cambro-Norman Surnames of Ireland
  www.rootsweb.com/~irlkik/ihm/irename2.htm
  List

- Old Irish-Gaelic Surnames
  www.rootsweb.com/~irlkik/ihm/irenames.htm

- Researching Irish Surnames
  www.rootsweb.com/~fianna/surname/

- Surnames Common in Ireland during the 16th century
  www.rootsweb.com/%7Efianna/surname/dhnames1.html

- Surnames in Ireland
  www.ajmorris.com/dig/toc/__01irsu.htm
  Pay per view site. Scanned pages from the book by Sir Robert E. Matheson, based on information from the indexes of the General Register Office

- Surnames: the correct spelling?
  www.from-ireland.net/gene/surnamedisc.htm

- Top 50 Irish Surnames
  www.genealogyforum.rootsweb.com/gfaol/surnames/Irish.htm
  Gateway to sites on specific surnames

- Using Distribution Studies to Identify the Place of Origin of your Irish Ancestors
  www.ajmorris.com/roots/ireland/dist.htm

- www.Irish Surnames.net
  freepages.genealogy.rootsweb.com/~irishancestors/
  Surnames__index.html

  General discussion

Cork

- Surnames of County Cork
  cork.local.ie/content/28107.shtm
  Surname history

Kilkenny
- Surnames of Co. Kilkenny
  www.rootsweb.com/~irlkik/ksurname.htm

Longford
- Surnames of County Longford
  longford.local.ie/content/28175.shtml
  Essay

Offaly
- Surnames of County Offaly
  offaly.local.ie/content/28150.shtml
  General discussion

Roscommon
- Roscommon Surnames
  www.rootsweb.com/~irlros/surnames.htm
  General discussion of surnames, with lists of common ones

Wexford
- Surnames of County Wexford
  wexford.local.ie/content/28164.shtml
  General discussion

United Irishmen
- Wicklow United Irishmen 1797-1804
  www.pcug.org.au/~ppmay/wicklow.htm

14. Professional Services, Booksellers, *etc.*

A. Professional Genealogists
If you want to employ a professional genealogist, you should first read:
- Employing a Professional Researcher: a practical guide
  www.sog.org.uk/leaflets/researcher.html

Many professional genealogists have their own web page. These are not listed here, but many can be found using gateways such as Cyndi's List (see below). The best way to locate a professional is to consult:
- Association of Professional Genealogists in Ireland
  indigo.ie/~apgi

See also:
- Irish Professional Genealogists
  indigo.ie/~gorry/ProGen.html
  List of members of the Association of Professional Genealogists in Ireland, and the Association of Ulster Genealogists and Record Agents

- I.G.S.I. Links: Professional Genealogist and Services Link
  www.rootsweb.com/~irish/links/profess.htm

- List of Genealogical and Historical Researchers
  www.nationalarchives.ie/gen__researchers.html
  Compiled by the National Archives of Ireland

- What's What in Irish Genealogy: Research Services
  indigo.ie/~gorry/Research.html

- Commercial Researchers
  proni.nics.gov.uk/research/searcher.htm
  At the Public Record Office of Northern Ireland

B. Booksellers and Other Suppliers

- Book Publications and Libraries
  www.tiara.ie/books.html
  Many links to publishers, booksellers, periodicals, newspapers, *etc.*

- What's What in Irish Genealogy: Publications
  indigo.ie/~gorry/Public.html
  World-wide listing of publishers, bookshops, magazines, and books

Abeshaus

- Abeshaus
  www.abeshaus.com/new/Genealogy/irish.htm
  Irish books and CD's in an American bookshop

Alan Godfrey

- Old Ordnance Survey Maps for Ireland
  www.alangodfreymaps.co.uk/ireland.htm
  Facsimile publisher's catalogue

Audio-Tapes

- Audio Tapes.com
  www.audiotapes.com/search2.asp?Search=Ireland
  Lists audio-tapes on Irish genealogy available

Books Ulster

- Books Ulster
  www.booksulster.com

Eneclann

- Eneclann
  www.eneclann.ie
  CD publishers

Fly Leaf Press

- Fly Leaf Press
  www.flyleaf.ie/
  Publishers of Irish genealogy books

Genfindit

- Vital Records from England, Scotland, Ireland and Australasia: Genfindit Online Ordering Service
  www.genfindit.com/
  For online birth, marriage and death certificates, census records, *etc.*

Irish Academic Press

- Irish Academic Press: Genealogy
  www.iap.ie/gene.htm
  Publishers

Irish Genealogical Foundation

- Irish Families
  www.irishroots.com
  Homepage of the Irish Genealogical Foundation, with details of books for sale and lending in the U.S., also *O'Lochlainn's journal of Irish families, etc.*

Irish Genealogy Books

- Irish Genealogy Books
  www.exploringfamilyorigins.com
  Publisher's site

Irish Roots

- Irish Roots
  www.genealogy-books.com/acart/agora.cgi?product=ireland
  Bookseller's catalogue

Morgan Publications

- Morgan and Ui Dhubhthaig Publications
  homepages.tesco.net/~morganpublications/morganpu.htm
  Includes many Irish books

Morris, Andrew J.

- Andrew J. Morris's Irish Family History and Genealogy
  www.ajmorris.com/a03/irfamhst.htm
  CD and fiche publisher

- Genealogical Resources from A.J.Morris: Genealogy Publications Catalog
  www.ajmorris.com/roots/catalog/

Quintin Publications
- Quintin Publications: Ireland Catalog
  www.quintinpublications.com/ireland.html

Seanchai Books
- Seanchai Books
  www.seanchaibooks.com
  Specialist in new and used Irish books

Ulster Historical Foundation Bookshop
- Ulster Historical Foundation Bookshop
  www.ancestryireland.com/cgi-bin/bookstore/main.pl

Subject Index

Institution Index

Place Index